Israel

Other Books of Related Interest:

Opposing Viewpoints Series

The Middle East Peace Process

At Issue Series

How Should the U.S. Proceed in Afghanistan?

Current Controversies Series

Iran

"Congress shall make
no law. . .abridging the
freedom of speech, or
of the press."

First Amendment to the U.S. Constitution

The basic foundation of our democracy is the First Amendment guarantee of freedom of expression. The *Opposing Viewpoints* Series is dedicated to the concept of this basic freedom and the idea that it is more important to practice it than to enshrine it.

OPPOSING
VIEWPOINTS®
SERIES

Israel

Myra Immell, Book Editor

GREENHAVEN PRESS
A part of Gale, Cengage Learning

GALE
CENGAGE Learning™

Detroit • New York • San Francisco • New Haven, Conn • Waterville, Maine • London

Christine Nasso, *Publisher*
Elizabeth Des Chenes, *Managing Editor*

© 2011 Greenhaven Press, a part of Gale, Cengage Learning.

Gale and Greenhaven Press are registered trademarks used herein under license.

For more information, contact:
Greenhaven Press
27500 Drake Rd.
Farmington Hills, MI 48331-3535
Or you can visit our Internet site at gale.cengage.com

For product information and technology assistance, contact us at

Gale Customer Support, 1-800-877-4253
For permission to use material from this text or product, submit all requests online at
www.cengage.com/permissions

Further permissions questions can be emailed to permissionrequest@cengage.com

Articles in Greenhaven Press anthologies are often edited for length to meet page requirements. In addition, original titles of these works are changed to clearly present the main thesis and to explicitly indicate the author's opinion. Every effort is made to ensure that Greenhaven Press accurately reflects the original intent of the authors. Every effort has been made to trace the owners of copyrighted material.

Cover Image copyright © Mazor/Dreamstime.com.

LIBRARY OF CONGRESS CATALOGING-IN-PUBLICATION DATA

Israel / Myra Immell, book editor.
    p. cm. -- (Opposing viewpoints)
    Includes bibliographical references and index.
    ISBN 978-0-7377-4974-8 (hardcover) -- ISBN 978-0-7377-4975-5 (pbk.)
    1. Arab-Israeli conflict. 2. Arab-Israeli conflict--1993--Peace. 3. Pacific settlement of international disputes. I. Immell, Myra.
    DS119.6.I72 2010
    956.04--dc22

                                    2010022999

Printed in the United States of America
1 2 3 4 5 6 7 14 13 12 11 10

Contents

Why Consider
Opposing Viewpoints?

> *"The only way in which a human being can make some approach to knowing the whole of a subject is by hearing what can be said about it by persons of every variety of opinion and studying all modes in which it can be looked at by every character of mind. No wise man ever acquired his wisdom in any mode but this."*
>
> John Stuart Mill

In our media-intensive culture it is not difficult to find differing opinions. Thousands of newspapers and magazines and dozens of radio and television talk shows resound with differing points of view. The difficulty lies in deciding which opinion to agree with and which "experts" seem the most credible. The more inundated we become with differing opinions and claims, the more essential it is to hone critical reading and thinking skills to evaluate these ideas. Opposing Viewpoints books address this problem directly by presenting stimulating debates that can be used to enhance and teach these skills. The varied opinions contained in each book examine many different aspects of a single issue. While examining these conveniently edited opposing views, readers can develop critical thinking skills such as the ability to compare and contrast authors' credibility, facts, argumentation styles, use of persuasive techniques, and other stylistic tools. In short, the Opposing Viewpoints Series is an ideal way to attain the higher-level thinking and reading skills so essential in a culture of diverse and contradictory opinions.

In addition to providing a tool for critical thinking, Opposing Viewpoints books challenge readers to question their own strongly held opinions and assumptions. Most people form their opinions on the basis of upbringing, peer pressure, and personal, cultural, or professional bias. By reading carefully balanced opposing views, readers must directly confront new ideas as well as the opinions of those with whom they disagree. This is not to simplistically argue that everyone who reads opposing views will—or should—change his or her opinion. Instead, the series enhances readers' understanding of their own views by encouraging confrontation with opposing ideas. Careful examination of others' views can lead to the readers' understanding of the logical inconsistencies in their own opinions, perspective on why they hold an opinion, and the consideration of the possibility that their opinion requires further evaluation.

Evaluating Other Opinions

To ensure that this type of examination occurs, Opposing Viewpoints books present all types of opinions. Prominent spokespeople on different sides of each issue as well as well-known professionals from many disciplines challenge the reader. An additional goal of the series is to provide a forum for other, less known, or even unpopular viewpoints. The opinion of an ordinary person who has had to make the decision to cut off life support from a terminally ill relative, for example, may be just as valuable and provide just as much insight as a medical ethicist's professional opinion. The editors have two additional purposes in including these less known views. One, the editors encourage readers to respect others' opinions—even when not enhanced by professional credibility. It is only by reading or listening to and objectively evaluating others' ideas that one can determine whether they are worthy of consideration. Two, the inclusion of such viewpoints encourages the important critical thinking skill of objectively evaluating an author's credentials and bias. This evaluation will illuminate an author's reasons for taking a particular stance on an issue and will aid in readers' evaluation of the author's ideas.

It is our hope that these books will give readers a deeper understanding of the issues debated and an appreciation of the complexity of even seemingly simple issues when good and honest people disagree. This awareness is particularly important in a democratic society such as ours in which people enter into public debate to determine the common good. Those with whom one disagrees should not be regarded as enemies but rather as people whose views deserve careful examination and may shed light on one's own.

Thomas Jefferson once said that "difference of opinion leads to inquiry, and inquiry to truth." Jefferson, a broadly educated man, argued that "if a nation expects to be ignorant and free . . . it expects what never was and never will be." As individuals and as a nation, it is imperative that we consider the opinions of others and examine them with skill and discernment. The Opposing Viewpoints Series is intended to help readers achieve this goal.

David L. Bender and Bruno Leone,
Founders

Introduction

> *"Were we to ask where the state of Israel is—where the borders are—we would never receive a simple answer. The borders of Israel are contested."*

> *Lev Luis Grinberg*

On November 29, 1947, the United Nations General Assembly took what turned out to be a momentous step. On this date they passed UN Resolution 181, which partitioned, or divided, the territory of the British Mandate of Palestine into two states—one Jewish and one Arab—and made Jerusalem an internationalized city. Jewish representatives in Palestine accepted the plan. Palestinian Arabs and the Arab League rejected it and formed volunteer armies that began to move into Palestine the month after the Resolution passed. This did not stop the Jews from recognizing their dream of an independent homeland, and on May 14, 1948, the State of Israel—Medinat Yisrael—declared its independence.

What started out as infiltration rapidly evolved into full-fledged war—the first Arab-Israeli War. Israelis call it the War of Independence; Arabs call it *Nakba*, or Catastrophe. In the view of some historians, it was one of the most important wars of the twentieth century. The Arabs were defeated, and the Palestinian state never really came into being. When the war ended in 1949, the Arab countries that had invaded Israel signed the 1949 Armistice, which spelled out the temporary borders between Israel and the Arab states. The border with Egypt was restored to its previous line, with the exception of the Gaza Strip, where Egypt continued in control. The borders with Lebanon and Syria also were restored to the previous lines. Jordan kept control of the Old City of Jerusalem and the hill country traditionally known as Judea and Samaria, newly named the "West Bank" (of the River Jordan). The result was that the territory UN Resolution 181 had allocated for the Palestinian state was taken over by Israel and Jordan. During the war and with the signing of the armistice, approximately 780,000 Palestinians fled the area and became refugees, mostly in other Arab lands.

During the cease-fire negotiations between Israel and Jordan, a line of demarcation was established between the two countries. That line, drawn roughly along the current boundary between Israel and the West Bank, is known as the "Green Line," the name it supposedly got because it originally was drawn on a map in green pen or pencil. The Green Line remained the boundary until 1967, when a third Arab-Israeli war resulted in a change that to this day remains a source of conflict.

That war, the Arab-Israel War of 1967, erupted between Israel and Egypt, Syria, Jordan, and Iraq. Issues that had contributed to or had arisen from the first two Arab-Israeli wars (in 1948 and 1956) had not been resolved to everyone's satisfaction. Among these were the Palestinian refugee problem, the borders between Israel and the Arab states, and the right of Israel to exist. The war lasted only six days. By its end Israel had captured and occupied the Gaza Strip, which had been under Egypt's administration since 1948; Egypt's Sinai Peninsula; Jordan's West Bank and East Jerusalem; and Syria's Golan Heights. This was enough territory to more than triple the size of the area Israel controlled. In an attempt to settle the conflict and bring peace, the United Nations Security Council called for Israel to withdraw from the occupied territories. The Arab states also demanded withdrawal. Israel did not comply.

In 1979, under a newly signed Israel-Egypt Peace Treaty, Israel returned the Sinai Peninsula to Egypt and began a three-year withdrawal from the area. In the early 1990s, a Palestinian National Authority was created to administer the West Bank and Gaza. Today, Israel still controls all of the Golan Heights, Gaza is an autonomous territory under the control of Hamas, the smaller of the two main Palestinian political parties, and the West Bank is ruled by Fatah, the larger of the two main Palestinian political parties, and the Israeli government.

The status of the occupied territories and the issue of the Israeli right to maintain hold of and build Jewish settlements in them is a major issue of debate worldwide—and of escalating Israeli-Palestinian conflict and violence. Complicating the issue is the fact that technically Israel has no legal, binding borders because the state of Israel has not established them. The Palestinians, among other groups and nations, believe the occupied territories should be returned to the Arabs and Israel's borders reverted back to the pre-1967 Green Line. The Israeli government and other groups disagree.

Israel and its neighbors are faced with complex issues— and increasing internal and external pressure to resolve them. Some of these issues, and the questions underlying them, are probed and debated in the following chapters: Should Israel Exist? What Are Key Issues of the Israeli-Palestinian Conflict? Is Peace Possible Between Israel and the Palestinians? and What Should U.S. Policy Be Toward Israel? Knowledge of how Israel came to occupy Arab territories and of Israel's borders in general is essential to the understanding of these issues and to an understanding of the ongoing conflict that has plagued Israel since its creation.

CHAPTER 1

Should Israel Exist?

Chapter Preface

Israel is a very small country—smaller than the state of New Jersey and about one-nineteenth the size of the state of California. When first declared a state in 1948, it was home to 806,000 people. By the next year, the population had reached 1 million. By 1958, it had grown to 2 million. By the end of January 2010, it had grown to approximately 7.5 million. Of that number, approximately 20 percent are Arabs and about 4 percent are immigrants and their children who are not registered as Jews by the Interior Ministry. The other approximately 75 percent of the population—in other words, the majority—are Jews, most of whom are of European-American extraction, with smaller numbers of African and Asian origins. Less than 35 percent are native-born Israelis with parents who were also born in Israel.

The overwhelming number of Jews is to be expected because Israel is a Jewish state, established as a national home for the Jewish people, a safe haven from which Jews worldwide could escape the anti-Semitism that resulted in the hostility, violence, and oppression to which they had been subjected for hundreds of years. The Law of Return, passed into law in 1950 by the Israeli Knesset, or parliament, along with the Law of Citizenship, gives every Jew in the world the right to settle in Israel as an automatic citizen. This encourages Jewish immigration and, along with it, continued survival of Israel as a Jewish state.

Much of the Arab world has refused to accept the legitimacy of Israel's creation and has opposed its existence since Israel was first declared a state. Over time, others also began to look suspiciously at Israel, at its actions and practices and laws, and to question its validity. In recent years, it is not just the existence of Israel as a Jewish state that is being questioned by some but the existence of Israel at all.

Western European media is filled with anti-Israel stories, articles, and editorials. Statements intended to undermine Israel's right to exist as a Jewish state are not uncommon. According to a 2007 article in *Haaretz*, a major Israeli newspaper, the questioning in Europe of Israel's right to exist "hides a definitive stance, which regards Israel as a passing colonial phenomenon and the Jewish people as an ethnic-religious group different from any other people and all other nation-states."

There is an increasingly successful move to delegitimize Israel by labeling as war crimes many of its efforts to combat terrorism and by charging that Israel is racist to the point of practicing apartheid, claiming that it grants numerous rights to its Jewish citizens while denying its Palestinian-Arab citizens the most basic freedoms. The movement to call Israel to account for its alleged crimes against the Palestinian people is growing, resulting in a gradual lessening of public support in the West for Israel.

Israel's existence is also being threatened by the more radical stance assumed by many of its Arab citizens, including Arab members of the Israeli government. According to Israeli historian Benny Morris, many openly embrace Palestinian national aims, give their loyalty to their people rather than to Israel, and call for autonomy and for the dissolution of the Jewish state.

Should Israel continue to exist as a Jewish nation? Should Israel continue to exist in its present form? Should Israel continue to exist at all? These three questions have become an increasingly popular and impassioned subject of debate in many countries, including Israel itself. The authors in the following chapter offer opposing viewpoints on the issue.

| "I say to the world, our very existence
per se is our right to exist!"

Israel Has a Right to Exist

Yehuda Avner

In the following viewpoint, Yehuda Avner illustrates how former Israeli prime minister Menachem Begin reacted to the idea that Israel needed affirmation of its right to exist. Begin argued that Israel's existence should not even be questioned, let alone have to be sanctioned for political purposes. Begin also asserts that Israel meets the four major criteria of statehood under international law and does exist.

Yehuda Avner served as adviser to five Israeli prime ministers and, in 1983, as Israeli ambassador to the United Kingdom.

As you read, consider the following questions:

1. According to Menachem Begin, as quoted by Avner, what four attributes qualify Israel as a fully fledged sovereign state?

2. In Begin's view, as cited by the author, why do the Jewish people not need anyone's recognition of their right to exist in Israel?

Yehuda Avner, "Israel Does Not Need Palestinian Recognition," *Jerusalem Post*, June 14, 2006, p. 13. Copyright © 2006 The Jerusalem Post. All rights reserved. Reproduced by permission. Yehuda Avner is also the author of the book *The Prime Ministers* (Toby Press), September 1, 2010.

3. Who does Avner quote Begin as saying is solely responsible for Israel's right to exist?

There is irony in the thought that were [former Israeli prime minister] Menachem Begin alive today he would be saddened, indeed outraged, at Prime Minister Ehud Olmert's insistence—in consort with the US and the EU [European Union]—that [Palestinian Islamic fundamentalist organization] Hamas's political legitimacy be conditioned, inter alia [among other things], on its recognition of Israel's right to exist.

"Right to exist?" I can hear the late prime minister roundly chastising his younger successor who declares himself to be a Begin disciple. "Are you telling me, Ehud, that our right to exist in Eretz Yisrael [the land of Israel] has to be sanctioned for political purposes by an intrinsically anti-Semitic, murderous Palestinian Arab terrorist organization? Have you lost your Jewish self-respect? Where is your Jewish memory?"

Menachem Begin had a surfeit of both—Jewish self-respect and memory. He had an all-encompassing grasp of Jewish history. Instinctively his memory went back thousands of years and his vision forward thousands of years. Jewish nostalgia fed his soul; it nurtured his deepest convictions.

Statehood as Defined by International Law

So when, on the first day of his premiership in 1977, he was waylaid by a tall, debonair, rakishly good-looking Englishman in a bow tie and a perfectly pitched BBC [British Broadcasting Company] announcer's voice, and saucily asked whether he looked forward to a time when the Palestinians would recognize Israel, his jaw tightened in restrained Jewish anger. But honed as he was by years of legal training, he answered with the composed demeanor of a practiced jurist, saying, "Traditionally, there are four major criteria of statehood under international law. One—an effective and independent government.

Two—an effective and independent control of the population. Three—a defined territory. And four—the capacity to freely engage in foreign relations. Israel is in possession of all four attributes and, hence, is a fully fledged sovereign state and a fully accredited member of the United Nations."

"But, surely, you would insist, would you not, that the relevant Palestinian organizations recognize Israel as a sine qua non [something essential] for negotiations with them?" persisted the fellow.

"Certainly not! Those so-called relevant organizations are gangs of murderers bent on destroying the State of Israel. We will never conduct talks about our own destruction."

"And were they to recognize Israel's existence—would you then negotiate with them?" pressed the correspondent.

"No, sir!"

"Why not?"

"Because I don't need Palestinian recognition for my right to exist."

Israel's Inalienable Right to Exist

Two hours later Menachem Begin stood at the podium of the Knesset [Israeli parliament], presenting his new cabinet. He began by dryly outlining the democratic processes that led to the changing of the guard, from [the] Labor [Party] to [the] Likud [Party]. And then, in recollection perhaps, of his acerbic exchange with the BBC man, he began talking about Israel's right to exist.

"Our right to exist—have you ever heard of such a thing?" he declared, passion creeping into his voice. "Would it enter the mind of any Briton or Frenchman, Belgian or Dutchman, Hungarian or Bulgarian, Russian or American, to request for its people recognition of its right to exist?"

He glared at his audience and wagged a finger, stilling every chattering voice in the Knesset chamber. And now, using his voice like a cello, sonorous and vibrant, he drove on:

Israel Needs No Recognition of Its Right to Exist

There are some governments which in a benevolent spirit, offer to secure the consent of the Arab states to the recognition of our right to exist. It is sometimes my duty to say that we do not ask any recognition of our right to exist, because our right to exist is independent of any recognition of it. An international community which can accommodate 127 sovereign states from Afghanistan to Zambia in alphabetical order, from Fiji to Albania in chronological order, with dozens of statehoods, not all of which have such a sharp identity of spiritual and cultural individualism as Israel: such a world community can accommodate a state of Israel within a few thousand square miles.

Abba Eban, Commonwealth Club, November 14, 1970.
www.commonwealthclub.org.

"Mr. Speaker: We were granted our right to exist by the God of our fathers at the glimmer of the dawn of human civilization four thousand years ago. Hence, the Jewish people have an historic, eternal and inalienable right to exist in this land, Eretz Yisrael, the land of our forefathers. We need nobody's recognition in asserting this inalienable right. And for this inalienable right, which has been sanctified in Jewish blood from generation to generation, we have paid a price un-exampled in the annals of nations."

Then he rose up on his toes, his shoulders squared, thumped the podium, and perorated in a voice that was thunder, "Mr. Speaker: From the Knesset of Israel, I say to the world, our very existence per se is our right to exist!"

A spontaneous applause rose from the benches. Many got to their feet in full-throated acclaim. It was a stirring Knesset moment—a moment of instinctive self-recognition affirming that though the State of Israel was then but 29 years old, its roots in Eretz Yisrael ran 4,000 years deep.

A Meeting with the American President

Three weeks later, the very same issue cropped up once more when Prime Minister Begin first met President Jimmy Carter in the White House. As their encounter drew to a close, the president handed the premier a piece of heavy bond White House stationery on which the formal communiqué to be released in their name was drafted.

"I trust this will meet with your approval," said Carter in his reedy Georgian voice.

Begin ran his eye over the one page text, and said, "Totally acceptable, Mr. President, but for one sentence."

Secretary of State Cyrus Vance, an unruffled man as a rule, who had invested much effort in drafting the document, became momentarily agitated. After a year at the job he had perfected a manner of drafting such joint statements designed to convey as little meaning as possible.

"And what might that be?" he asked.

"Please delete the sentence which reads, 'The United States affirms Israel's inherent right to exist.'"

President Carter's steely pale-blue eyes flared in surprise. "It would be incompatible with my responsibilities as president of the United States were I to omit this commitment to your country," he said. "To the best of my knowledge, every Israeli prime minister has asked for this public pledge."

An Absolute Given: Israel's Right to Exist

"I sincerely appreciate you sentiment, Mr. President," said Mr. Begin, his tone deeply reflective as if reaching down into generations of memory, "But it would be equally incompatible with my responsibilities as prime minister of Israel were I not to ask you to erase that sentence."

"But why?"

"Because our Jewish state needs no American affirmation of our right to exist. Our Hebrew bible established that right millennia ago. Never, throughout the centuries, did we ever abandon or forfeit that right. Therefore, sir, we alone, the Jewish people—no one else—are responsible for our country's right to exist."

So yes, Menachem Begin would, indeed, have had that to say to Ehud Olmert, were he around today. Never would he have put on the table a demand for recognition of Israel's right to exist as a quid pro quo for negotiation. To him, this was a high ideological principle, a fundamental axiom, an absolute given, a natural corollary of his all-embracing view of Jewry's extraordinary history.

Ehud, take it out.

▌ *"Israel does not have the right to exist."*

Israel Has No Right to Exist

David Wearing

In the following viewpoint, David Wearing argues that philosophically states do not have a right to exist. A state is only justified in so far as it serves the purpose of safeguarding peoples' human rights, Wearing maintains. According to the author, Israel has deprived Palestinians of their basic human right to live in peace and security and with full self-determination. Given this, Wearing asserts, Israel has no "right" to continue to exist.

David Wearing is working for a PhD in political science at University College, London, specializing in British foreign policy. His articles have been published by the Guardian *and* Le Monde Diplomatique.

As you read, consider the following questions:

1. According to Wearing, why should Palestinians not acknowledge that Israel has a right to exist?

2. What principle has been forgotten by those who talk about Israel's right to exist, according to the author?

3. According to Wearing, in the case of Israel and the Palestinians, to what have the rights of people been subordinated?

David Wearing, "Israel's 'Right' to Exist," *The Democrat's Diary*, February 4, 2009. Reproduced by permission.

A commenter on my last post draws attention to the political platform of the Israeli Likud party, likely winners of next week's legislative elections. According to information on the Knesset (Israeli Parliment) web site (which I assume reflects the current position), Likud still opposes the establishment of a Palestinian state.

Recall that when the Palestinians in the occupied territories elected Hamas to power in January 2006, Israel and its Western allies instituted a boycott against the territories on the basis that, amongst other pretexts, one cannot enter into dialogue with a group—Hamas—that doesn't recognise the "right" of Israel to exist. That boycott turned into a blockade, condemned by leading aid agencies, which created a humanitarian disaster in the Gaza strip, with children becoming malnourished and people dying from lack of medical treatment. All because Hamas' alleged extremism rendered it *persona non grata* at the high table of international diplomacy.

Put aside the fact that Hamas has long accepted the reality of Israel's existence, dismissing the idea of doing otherwise as "infantile". Put aside the fact that for Palestinians to go further than merely accepting Israel's existence—for them to say that Israel has the "right" to exist—would mean them accepting that it was "right" for hundreds of thousands of Palestinians to have been subjected to the brutal ethnic cleansing operation that brought the creation of the Israeli state on the ashes of the former Palestinian homeland.

Put all that aside and just consider the sheer, rampant hypocrisy. Israeli Leaders (not just Likud) have consistently denied Palestine's "right to exist" as an equal state alongside Israel, not just in word but—crucially, given the vast power imbalance—in deed. Despite this, no supporter of Palestinian national rights would argue that the Palestinians should refuse to negotiate and agree to a peaceful settlement with the elected Israeli government. This illustrates pretty clearly, I think, which side of this debate has a genuine interest in peace and which side clings to flimsy excuses to avoid it.

It's worth saying something else about the "right to exist". Israel does not have the right to exist, and neither does Palestine. Things do not have rights, people have rights. My laptop, my biro, my tea cup, do not have rights. They, like states, have uses which they either do or do not serve successfully.

Jews and Arabs have the equal right as human beings to live in peace and security and with full self-determination. Whatever set-up you have in former Mandate Palestine—a Jewish and an Arab state side by side, a single democratic state for both peoples—is only justified in so far as it serves the purpose of safeguarding those human rights. The current set-up—an Israeli state that confers racial privilege on its Jewish over its Arab inhabitants, with the rest of the Palestinians either locked into dungeon-like conditions in modern day Indian reservations, or exiled altogether—has no justification in terms of any recognisable concept of "rights".

Those who talk about Israel's "right" to exist have forgotten a principle—that states are entirely subordinate to human rights—which has been understood by democrats for centuries.

Over two hundred years ago, the American founding fathers, when articulating the fundamental principles of democracy, said that:

"We hold these truths to be sacred and undeniable; that all men are created equal and independent, that from that equal creation they derive rights inherent and inalienable, among which are the preservation of life, and liberty, and the pursuit of happiness; that to secure these ends, governments are instituted among men, deriving their just powers from the consent of the governed; that *whenever any form of government shall become destructive of these ends, it is the right of the people to alter or to abolish it, and to institute new government,* laying it's foundation on such principles and organising it's powers in such form, as to them shall seem most likely to effect their safety and happiness." [my emphasis]

According to these principles, it is quite legitimate to consider the abolition of the state of Israel, if that is what "shall seem most likely to effect [the] safety and happiness" of the Jews and Arabs of the region. There is no "right" for a state to persist in circumstances where it presents an obstacle to the honouring of basic human rights. As it happens, I don't support calls for the abolition of the state of Israel. But the principles at work here need to be understood.

The idea that a state has the "right to exist" directly contradicts the principles set forth by the early democrats in their struggles against the monarchical tyrannies of the late 18th and early 19th centuries. The man who led the intellectual counter-charge against democracy, Edmund Burke, said:

"The occupation of the hairdresser or of a working tallow-chandler cannot be a matter of honour to any person . . . Such descriptions of men ought not to suffer oppression from the state; *but the state suffers oppression if such as they . . . are permitted to rule*" (Simon Schama's "History of Britian III", pg. 43).

Consider the value-system set out here by Burke. The danger of the state oppressing the population must be balanced against the danger of the *population* oppressing *the state*.

Those who reject negotiations with Hamas to help end the Israeli-Palestinian conflict, on the basis that Hamas rejects Israel's "right" to exist, are—in moral terms—taking the same backward, anti-democratic position as Edmund Burke two-hundred years ago, when he defended the old monarchies of Europe against the threat of the "swinish multitude". The rights of people are subordinated to the alleged "rights" of the state. The right of the Palestinians for their desperate situation to be resolved, so they can live decent lives free from hunger, poverty and violence, is subordinated to the "right" of the Israeli state to exist in whatever form it chooses, whatever the human cost, and to have that "right" affirmed by its victims. Until the Palestinians bow down before the fake "rights" of the Israeli state, their actual rights will continue to be denied to them.

Israel likes to present itself as a bulwark of enlightened Western democracy, resisting the advances of the swarthy Islamic hordes. In reality, the Israeli state, and those who would see Palestinian lives sacrificed on the altar of its "right" to exist, are the moral equivalent of the pre-Enlightenment reactionaries of monarchical 18th century Europe. The barbarism of Israel's recent massacres in Gaza is partially an outcome of the perverse morality that subordinates the rights of human beings to the "rights" of a state.

| "The right of the Arab minority to equality ... cannot lead us to hesitate in our insistence on preserving the state's definition as 'Jewish.'"

Israel Needs to Remain a Jewish State

Avi Sagi and Yedidia Stern

In the following viewpoint, Avi Sagi and Yedidia Stern contend that Arab Israelis are challenging the right of the Jewish majority of Israel to maintain a Jewish nation-state. They argue that the Arab vision of Israel as a multicultural state will not work and that Israel must retain its Jewish identity.

Avi Sagi is a professor in the Department of Philosophy at Israel's Bar-Ilan University and a senior research fellow at Shalom Hartman Institute in Jerusalem. Yedidia Stern is vice president for research on the Jewish state at Israel Democracy Institute in Jerusalem and a professor at Bar-Ilan University Law School.

As you read, consider the following questions:

1. According to Sagi and Stern, what change are the Arabs demanding in public spaces?

2. According to the authors, what will happen if the State of Israel is voided of identity components?

3. Why is the Israeli Arab demand for equality in the public space intolerable, according to Sagi and Stern?

The wheel comes full circle. Not long ago, we sinned by asserting lordship—"There is no Palestinian people." Over the years this view was shorn from the marketplace of ideas of the Jewish majority in Israel, and we no longer reject the national identity of these others. Now however, leading figures among Israel's Arab community are paying us back in a similar coin: Several recently published documents laying out their vision for the future call for the annulment of the Jewish identity of the State of Israel, from which it follows that they are rejecting a central element of identity of the Jewish people in our generation. This is a strategic move by a substantial portion of the leadership of about a fifth of the country's citizens, and it should be taken seriously.

An Assault on Israel's Jewish Character

We pushed the Arab citizens into an alley with no exit: they are experiencing prolonged discrimination that cannot be justified. Their right to full civil equality is not being realized. Decent Israelis cannot remain silent in the light of the state's ongoing failure in its treatment of the minority group. Moreover, decent Jews cannot ignore their responsibility to protect the national minority from manifestations of racism. We did not make an effort to consolidate civil partnership; we did not create inviting conditions for honorable coexistence. The outcry of the poor Arab, who is discriminated against as a person and who feels excluded and alienated as the member of a minority group, is resonating across the country. It raises doubts about the depth of our true commitment to the values of a "Jewish state" and a "democratic state."

However, the new initiatives of the Arab leadership in Israel are not making do with a call to rectify the wrongs done to the minority. The central innovation of principle in these documents lies in their categorical assertion that proper equality will not be achieved as long as Israel is a Jewish state. Accordingly, they launch a frontal assault against the state's Jewish character. If the previous generation of Arabs, the "stooped generation," was content to aspire to civil equality, the present "erect generation" is challenging the right of the majority to maintain a Jewish nation-state.

A Conspiracy of Elites

The broad context of the "Future Vision" document[1] arises clearly from its opening lines. The reproof sticks out like thorns in one's eyes: "Israel is the outcome of a settlement process initiated by the Zionist-Jewish elite in Europe and the West and realized by colonial countries." The voice that is speaking here is none other than the National Committee for the Heads of the Arab Local Authorities in Israel. These people, Israeli public representatives who live in close proximity to us Jews, believe that the State of Israel is not the realization of generations of Jewish longing to return to Zion, but a conspiracy by elites seeking to impose Western control over the Middle East. "Next year in Jerusalem, As long as deep in the heart ... My heart is in the East and I am at the ends of the West"—[according to them] none of these are authentic expressions of the Jewish soul across the generations.

This is historical nonsense. Postcolonial theories cannot transform a full life into a fiction. Even those who feel victimized by the Nakba[2] cannot erase the fact that "The Land of Israel was the birthplace of the Jewish people. Here their spiritual, religious and political identity was shaped," as Israel's

1. "The Future Vision of the Palestinian Arabs in Israel" was issued in 2006. The document defines the Israeli-Palestinian vision of changes needed to bring about the kind of society they could live in with dignity.

2. The Arabic term *Nakba*, meaning "catastrophe," is used by the Palestinians to refer to the flight and expulsion of Palestinian Arabs in 1948 and the defeat of the Arab armies in the 1948 Arab-Israeli War.

A Baseless Attack on Israel

Equally remarkable, for all the singular focus on Israel, the attack on Jewish statehood avoids even the slightest consideration of the specifics of Israel's case. The attackers fail to examine the legal or political consequences of Israel's national expression as a Jewish state (perhaps because they find none) with regard to its non-Jews, religious and racial equality, or the civil and political equality of all citizens. They also ignore the specific historical circumstances and perils that gave rise to the need for Israel to identify Jewishly. In short, it is an attack on Israel without regard to the cost, benefit, or uniqueness of Jewish statehood—indeed, without any grounding at all.

Dore Gold and Jeff Helmreich, Jerusalem Viewpoints, *November 16, 2003. www.jcpa.org.*

Declaration of Independence states. Israel's Arabs lose our attention if they refuse to recognize the fact that, as the declaration states, "After being forcibly exiled from their land, the people kept faith with it throughout their dispersion, and never ceased to pray and hope for their return to it and for the restoration in it of their political freedom. We are not strangers in our homeland."

The Arab Vision of a Multicultural State

The Arabs' visions also offer concrete solutions. They are striving to shape Israel as a multicultural state. However, the Arab leadership is not content with protecting certain public spaces, which are populated largely by members of the Arab minority, as areas in which Arab culture and identity will be embodied. They want much more. They are demanding that all the elements of the Israeli space—sovereignty, territory, norms and symbols—be freed of any specific identity. They are unwilling to make do with the rights accruing to a cultural minority. They want the Jewish majority to narrow its identity and apply it only in sub-state spaces. The state will be a neutral playing field, transparent and hollow, possessing a universal character.

An attempt to fashion a multicultural state of this kind will not succeed. History shows that multiculturalism has blossomed only when it is cultivated in a stable national-political space. The leadership of Israel's Arabs is seeking what no one had dared call for: for the overwhelming majority of the country's citizens to withdraw their collective identity to outside the public space, which is so vital to realize identity. In the absence of another Jewish state, the import of their demand will be to dwarf and diminish Jewish identity in our generation to its private and community dimensions, just as it was for two thousand years, when we were a people in exile.

Moreover, states need a unifying national ethos. Without it, a state is liable to become a random federation of communities that will find it difficult to exist as a homogeneous unit. This is even more acute in the Israeli context. The Arab minority is tied to social-cultural communities that exist in the Arab states and it is part of the Palestinian nation, which is in the process of establishing an independent state abutting on Israel. Is it far-fetched to be concerned that the Arab minority is actually interested in a two-state plan: voiding the existing ethos and replacing it, when the time comes, with a different national vision that will integrate into Arab or Islamic visions that are shared by the rest of the Palestinian nation, across the border?

If the State of Israel is voided of identity components, it will lose one of the crucial elements of national resilience which [secures] its continued existence in a hostile arena. Will Israeli youngsters—to whom the whole world is open—

respond to a mobilization call that asks them to give up their best years, and sometimes also their very lives, for an organizational framework that does not provide them with meaning? The internal centrifugal forces will make us fall apart from within, and the opportunities that beckon in the global village will hasten the process from without.

Behind the Multicultural Rhetoric

The suspicion arises that behind the multicultural rhetoric lies the aspiration to liquidate Israel as a political entity: Implicit in it is the ouster of the Jewish nation from the world's nations. Academic language possessing political charm might turn out to be a weapon in the struggle against the State of Israel. The Arab elite is leading its followers into dangerous realms. They must understand that the members of the Jewish people, including the salient supporters of civil equality for all, will not forgo the realization of their right to self-determination in this space, the cradle of the Jewish nation. The Jewish people has an inalienable right to the existence of the State of Israel as a Jewish state.

Israel's Arab citizens have to demand—and the Jewish majority must agree to—a fair division of the public space between the two groups. The Jewish majority will have the larger part of the realization of identity in this space, and the Arab minority will be left with the smaller part. Any other alternative will undermine, and ultimately void of content, the concepts of identity that underlie multiculturalism.

However, not all the public assets are amenable to division between majority and minority. Thus, for example, the definition of the state's character as "Jewish," to which the documents of the Arab vision object, is indivisible. This is the source of the argument that the right of the Arab minority to equality in the public space is infringed upon. Even though this is true, it cannot lead us to hesitate in our insistence on preserving the state's definition as "Jewish."

[British philosopher and historian] Isaiah Berlin stated that "[equality] is neither more nor less rational than any other ultimate principle." The basic point of departure of a liberal society is that equality is the primary value that must be applied, but it is possible to depart from this value if there is sufficient cause. Indeed, in Berlin's view, the majority of social disputes are related to the question of the nature of the sufficient cause to depart from equality.

An Intolerable Demand

As we noted, the demand of the Arab minority for civil equality is meritorious because no sufficient cause to justify its rejection is posited against it. In contrast, their demand for equality in the public space, to be achieved by removing the collective identity of more than three-quarters of the country's citizens from the sovereign space, is intolerable. Posited against it are extremely cogent sufficient causes, above all the discrimination against the Jewish national identity (vis-a-vis either national identities which find expression in a political space, including the Arab identities) and the degeneration it is liable to suffer as a result. To this we must add the concrete concern that the Israeli political state will be disassembled into unconnected sub-units, and the danger that strategic harm will accrue to national resilience.

The Arab public in Israel would do well to direct its energy to a struggle for civil equality, in which it will find many partners among the Jewish people. But continuing to build verbal sandcastles in the form of documents of the vision is pointless. The Jewish people does not intend to divest itself of its aspiration to realize its nationhood in the political space of the State of Israel.

| *"As an egalitarian argument we should say loud and clear that Israel has no right to exist as a Jewish state."*

Israel Must Not Remain a Jewish State

Oren Ben-Dor

In the following viewpoint, Oren Ben-Dor argues that as a Jewish state Israel does not treat all its citizens equally. It exists more for the sake of those considered Jewish than for that of those who are not, according to Ben-Dor. He contends that Israel's right to exist as a Jewish state should not be recognized, and that doing so will perpetuate inequalities and injustices and lead to more violence and bloodshed.

Oren Ben-Dor is a lecturer in law at the University of Southampton in the United Kingdom and lecturer of legal and political philosophy at Southampton University School of Law.

As you read, consider the following questions:

1. According to Ben-Dor, what are Palestinians being asked to recognize?

2. What does the Right of Return of Palestinians mean according to the author?

3. What does Ben-Dor mean by "a spirit of generosity" and what does he believe it will take for that spirit to be established?

Yet again, the Annapolis [, Maryland, site of the 2007 Middle East peace conference] meeting between [Israeli prime minister Ehud] Olmert and [Palestinian president Mahmoud] Abbas is preconditioned upon the recognition by the Palestinian side of the right of Israel to exist as a Jewish state. Indeed the "road map" should lead to, and legitimate, once and for all, the right of such a Jewish state to exist in definitive borders and in peace with its neighbours. The vision of justice, both past and future, simply has to be that of two states, one Palestinian, one Jewish, which would coexist side by side in peace and stability. Finding a formula for a reasonably just partition and separation is still the essence of what is considered to be moderate, pragmatic and fair ethos.

A Sacred Status

Thus, the really deep issues—the "core"—are conceived as the status of Jerusalem, the fate and future of the Israeli settlements in the Occupied Territories[1] and the viability of the future Palestinian state beside the Jewish one. The fate of the descendants of those 750000 Palestinians who were ethnically cleansed in 1948 from what is now, and would continue to be under a two-state solution, the State of Israel, constitutes a "problem" but never an "issue" because, God forbid, to make it an issue on the table would be to threaten the existence of Israel as a Jewish state. The existence of Israel as a Jewish state must never become a core issue. That premise unites political opinion in the Jewish state, ... and also persists as a pragmatic view of many Palestinians who would prefer some improvement to no improvement at all. Only "extremists" such

1. Territory captured by Israel from Egypt, Jordan, and Syria during the Six-Day War of 1967.

as [Palestinian Islamic fundamentalist organization] Hamas, anti-Semites, and Self-Hating Jews . . . can make Israel's existence into a core problem and in turn into a necessary issue to be debated and addressed.

The Jewish state, a supposedly potential haven for all the Jews in the world in the case a second Holocaust comes about, should be recognised as a fact on the ground blackmailed into the "never again" rhetoric. All considerations of pragmatism and reasonableness in envisioning a "peace process" to settle the 'Israeli/Palestinian' conflict must never destabilise the sacred status of that premise that a Jewish state has a right to exist.

Notice, however, that Palestinians are not asked merely to recognise the perfectly true fact and with it, the absolutely feasible moral claim, that millions of Jewish people are now living in the State of Israel and that their physical existence, liberty and equality should be protected in any future settlement. They are not asked merely to recognise the assurance that any future arrangement would recognise historic Palestine as a home for the Jewish People. What Palestinians are asked to subscribe to is recognition of the right of an ideology that informs the make-up of a state to exist as Jewish one. They are asked to recognise that ethno-nationalistic premise of statehood.

The fallacy is clear: the recognition of the right of Jews who are there . . . to remain there under liberty and equality in a post-colonial political settlement, is perfectly compatible with the non-recognition of the state whose constitution gives those Jews a preferential stake in the polity [state]. . . .

A Jewish State Defined

So let us boldly ask: What exactly is entailed by the requirement to recognise Israel as a Jewish state? What do we recognise and support when we purchase a delightful avocado or a date from Israel or when we invite Israel to take part in an international football event? What does it mean to be a friend of Israel? What precisely is that Jewish state whose status as such would be once and for all legitimised by . . . a two-state solution?

A Jewish state is a state which exists more for the sake of whoever is considered Jewish according to various ethnic, tribal, religious criteria, than for the sake of those who do not pass this test. What precisely are the criteria of the test for Jewishness is not important. . . . Instigating violence provides them with the impetus for doing that. What is significant, though, is that a test of Jewishness is being used in order to constitutionally protect . . . the differential ownership of a polity. A recognition of Israel's right to exist as a Jewish state is a recognition of the Jews special entitlement, as eternal victims, to have a Jewish state. Such a test of supreme stake for Jews is the supreme criterion not only for racist policy making by the legislature but also for a racist constitutional interpretation by the Supreme Court. The idea of a state that is first and foremost for the sake of Jews trumps even that basic law of Human Freedom and Dignity to which the Israeli Supreme Court pays so much lip service. Such constitutional interpretation would have to make the egalitarian principle equality of citizenship compatible with, and thus subservient to, the need to maintain the Jewish majority and character of the state. This of course constitutes a serious compromise of equality, translated into many individual manifestations of oppression and domination of those victims of such compromise—non-Jews-Arabs citizens of Israel.

Lack of Equality for Non-Jews

In our world, a world that resisted Apartheid South Africa so impressively, recognition of the right of the Jewish state to exist is a litmus test for moderation and pragmatism. The demand is that Palestinians recognise Israel's entitlement to constitutionally entrench a system of racist basic laws and policies, differential immigration criteria for Jews and non-Jews, differential ownership and settlements rights, differential capital investments, differential investment in education, formal rules and informal conventions that differentiate the potential stakes of political participation, lame-duck academic freedom and debate.

In the Jewish state of Israel non-Jews-Arabs citizens are just "bad luck" and are considered a ticking demographic bomb of "enemy within". They can be given the right to vote—indeed one member one vote—but the potential of their political power, even their birth rate, should be kept at bay by visible and invisible, instrumental and symbolic, discrimination. But now they are asked to put up with their inferior stake and recognise the right of Israel to continue to legitimate the non-egalitarian premise of its statehood. . . .

The Jewish state could only come into being in May 1948 by ethnically cleansing most of the indigenous population. . . . The judaisation of the state could only be effectively implemented by constantly internally displacing the population of many villages within the Israeli state.

The Right of Return of Jews

It would be unbearable and unreasonable to demand Jews to allow for the Right of Return of those descendants of the expelled. Presumably, those descendants too could go to a viable Palestinian state rather than, for example, rebuild their ruined village in the Galilee. On the other hand, a Jewish young couple from Toronto who never set their foot in Palestine has a right to settle in the Galilee. Jews and their descendants hold this right in perpetuity. You see, that right "liberates" them as people. Jews must never be put under the pressure to live as a substantial minority in the Holy Land under egalitar-

The Right to Carry Out Ethnic Cleansing

"Jewish state" means that Israel has an inherent right to discriminate against its non-Jewish citizens, especially the sizeable Palestinian minority, and, if need be expel them from the country in order to preserve the "Jewishness" of Israel.

In other words, Israel simply wants to obtain from the Palestinian leadership a recognition that it has a legal and moral right to carry out ethnic cleansing of its Christian and Muslim citizens on the ground that Israel is and must always remain a Jewish state.

Khalid Amayreh, Ikhwanweb, December 9, 2007.
www.ikhwanweb.com.

ian arrangement. Their past justifies their preferential stake and the preservation of their numerical majority in Palestine. . . .

It is clear that part of the realisation of that right of return would not only be just the actual return, but also the assurance of equal stake and citizenship of all, Jews and non-Jews-Arabs after the return. A return would make the egalitarian claim by those who return even more difficult to conceal than currently with regard to Israel Arab second class citizens. What unites Israelis and many world Jews behind the call for the recognition of the right of a Jewish state to exist is their aversion for the possibility of living, as a minority, under conditions of equality of stake to all. But if Jews enjoys this equality in Canada why can not they support such equality in Palestine through giving full effect to the right of Return of Palestinians?

The Right of Return of Palestinians

Let us look precisely at what the pragmatic challenge consists of: not pragmatism that entrenches inequality but pragmatism that responds to the challenge of equality.

The Right of Return of Palestinians means that Israel acknowledges and apologises for what it did in 1948. It does mean that Palestinian memory of the 1948 catastrophe, the Nakbah[2], is publicly revived in the Geography and collective memory of the polity. It does mean that Palestinians descendants would be allowed to come back to their villages. If this is not possible because there is a Jewish settlement there, they should be given the choice to found an alternative settlement nearby. This may mean some painful compulsory state purchase of agricultural lands that should be handed back to those who return. In cases when this is impossible they ought to be allowed the choice to settle in another place in the larger area or if not possible in another area in Palestine. Compensation would be the last resort and would always be offered as a choice. This kind of moral claim of return would encompass all Palestine including Tel Aviv.

At no time, however, would it be on the cards to throw Israeli Jews from their land. An egalitarian and pragmatic realisation of the Right of Return constitutes an egalitarian legal revolution. As such it would be paramount to address Jews' worries about security and equality in any future arrangement in which they, or any other group, may become a minority. Jews national symbols and importance would be preserved. . . .

But it is important to emphasise that the Palestinian Right of Return would mean that what would cease to exist is the premise of a Jewish as well as indeed a Muslim state. A return without the removal of the constitutionally enshrined preferential stake is return to serfdom.

2. The Arabic term Nakbah, meaning "catastrophe," is used by the Palestinians to refer to the flight and expulsion of Palestinian Arabs in 1948 and the defeat of the Arab armies in the 1948 Arab-Israeli War.

Non-Recognition of the Jewish State

The upshot is that only by individuating cases of injustice, by extending claims for injustice to all historic Palestine, by fair address of them without creating another injustice for Jews and finally by ensuring the elimination of all racist laws that stem from the Jewish nature of the state, including that nature itself, would justice be, and with it peace, possible. What we need is a spirit of generosity that is pragmatic but also morally uncompromising in terms of geographic ambit of the moral claims for repatriation and equality. This vision would propel the establishment of a Truth and Reconciliation Commission. But for all this to happen we must start by ceasing to recognize the right [of] Israel to exist as a Jewish state. No spirit of generosity would be established without an egalitarian call for jettisoning the ethno-nationalistic notion upon which the Jewish state is based. . . .

The non-recognition of the Jewish state is an egalitarian imperative that looks both at the past and to the future. It is the uncritical recognition of the right of Israel to exist as a Jewish state which is the core hindrance for this egalitarian premise to shape the ethical challenge that Palestine poses. A recognition of Israel's right to exist as a Jewish state means the silencing that would breed more and more violence and bloodshed. . . .

We must see that the uncritically accepted recognition of Israel's right to exist is . . . to accept Israel['s] claim to have the right to be racist or . . . to have the right to occupy, to dispossess and to discriminate. . . .

As an egalitarian argument we should say loud and clear that Israel has no right to exist as a Jewish state.

Periodical Bibliography

The following articles have been selected to supplement the diverse views presented in this chapter.

Ben Ehrenreich   "Zionism Is the Problem," *Los Angeles Times*, March 15, 2009.

Georgie Anne Geyer   "One-State Solution Hints," *Washington Times*, February 4, 2009.

Russell Nieli   "The Marriage of a One-State and a Two-State Solution," *Tikkun*, July–August 2009.

Michael B. Oren   "Seven Existential Threats," *Commentary*, May 2009.

Palestine Times   "Why Palestinians Should Never Recognize Israel's 'Right to Exist,'" April 4, 2007.

David Singer   "The Jewish State of Israel," *Arutz Sheva/Israel National News*, August 6, 2009.

Yonatan Touval   "A Recognition Israel Doesn't Need," *New York Times*, May 12, 2009.

Robin Yassin-Kassab   "Four Solutions for Palestine, Israel," *The Palestine Chronicle*, February 16, 2009.

Mortimer B. Zuckerman   "Reaffirming the Right of Israel to Exist in the Face of Hamas Attacks in Gaza; The Only Thing Hamas Likes Better than Dead Israelis Is Dead Palestinians," *U.S. News & World Report*, January 15, 2009.

OPPOSING
VIEWPOINTS®
SERIES

CHAPTER 2

What Are Key Issues of the Israeli-Palestinian Conflict?

Chapter Preface

"Everybody sees a difficulty in the question of relations between Arabs and Jews. But not everybody sees that there is no solution to this question. No solution! There is a gulf, and nothing can bridge it. . . . We as a nation want this country to be ours; the Arabs, as a nation, want this country to be theirs." These words, spoken in 1919 by a young Zionist politician named David Ben-Gurion, continue to ring true. At the heart of the decades-long Arab-Israeli conflict is disagreement between Jews and Arabs over who owns the land of Palestine, the pocket of land on the eastern Mediterranean surrounded by Egypt, Saudi Arabia, Jordan, Syria, and Lebanon.

For more than four hundred years—from the early 1500s until the early 1900s—the Ottoman Turks ruled Palestine. Their rule came to an end during World War I when they were defeated by the British. In 1915, in a document known as the Husayn-McMahon correspondence, the British promised the Arabs an independent country, which the Arabs believed would include all of Palestine. Two years later, in 1917, another document—the Balfour Declaration—announced that the British Government viewed "with favor the establishment in Palestine of a national home for the Jewish people." That same year Palestine was granted to Britain as a League of Nations mandate.

Meanwhile, large-scale Jewish immigration to Palestine, begun in the 1800s, continued to grow. By the late 1930s, almost one-third of Palestine's population was Jewish. The Arabs railed against the Jews coming in to take their land. To stem the riots and the revolts, the British limited Jewish immigration to Palestine. World War II (1939–1945) and the Holocaust brought new pressures, and the British found it increasingly difficult to control Jewish immigration to Palestine. At the same time, their efforts to stem the conflict between the Arabs and the Jews proved futile. In 1947, seeking an end to their mandate, they solicited help from the United Nations.

The United Nations response was to partition Palestine into an Arab state and a Jewish state. The Jewish state would have 56 percent of the territory, more than half of which was desert, and the Arabs 43 percent. Jerusalem would be run under an international UN administration. The Jews accepted the partition; the Arabs in Palestine and the Arab states did not.

On May 14, 1948, the Jews declared the state of Israel. The next day troops from neighboring Arab countries invaded, only to be defeated by the Israelis and lose land to them. Hundreds of thousands of Palestinians fled their homes, creating a massive refugee problem that continued to grow as more wars were fought and more Arab territory was lost to the Israelis.

Since 1948, there have been four more major Arab-Israeli wars, as well as continuous unrest and violence. Conflict continues to fester and, in spite of many efforts, there has been little compromise and even less resolution. Each side still has its own version of the same history, and each continues to claim that the conflict is not their fault and they are not the ones refusing to compromise. Each offers compelling arguments to support their beliefs. Although some Israelis and Palestinians profess they want an end to the conflict, there remains a lack of trust between most Jews and Arabs. The viewpoints in this chapter reveal the strength of the convictions held today about the primary cause of the conflict—the claim of both Arabs and Jews to the same land—as well as such other key issues as the Israeli treatment of Palestinian Arab citizens of Israel and the Palestinian refugees' right of return.

> "If any nation on earth has a right to
> any land—a right based on history, at-
> tachment, long association—then the
> Jewish people has a right to Israel."

Israel Rightfully Belongs to the Jews

Jonathan Sacks

In the following viewpoint, Jonathan Sacks argues that no one has a greater right to the land of Israel than the Jews. He maintains that they were the land's original inhabitants and have a connection with Israel that goes back thousands of years. No matter how many efforts were made over the years to deny the Jews the land promised them by God, Sacks asserts, they never left of their own free will or gave up their rights. Furthermore, according to Sacks, they were the first people ever to create and develop an independent state there.

Jonathan Sacks is chief rabbi of the United Hebrew Congregations of the British Commonwealth.

As you read, consider the following questions:

1. According to Sacks, when did the Jewish connection with Israel begin?

Jonathan Sacks, "Our Right to Israel Could Not Be More Powerful," *The Jewish Chronicle*, January 18, 2008. Reproduced by permission.

2. What did the Balfour Declaration attempt to do, according to the author?

3. According to Sacks, what have the Jews achieved in Israel?

My great-grand-father, Rabbi Arye Leib Frumkin, went to Israel in 1871; his father had settled there 20 years earlier. His first act was to begin writing his History of the Sages in Jerusalem, chronicling the Jewish presence there since Nachmanides arrived in 1265.

In 1881 pogroms [violent persecution of Jews] broke out in more than 100 towns in Russia. That was when he realised that aliyah [immigration of Jews to the Holy Land] was no longer a pilgrimage of the few but an urgent necessity for the many. He became a pioneer, moving to one of the first agricultural settlements in the new yishuv [Jewish community in Palestine before Israel's statehood]. The early settlers had caught malaria and left. Rabbi Frumkin led the return and built the first house there. The name they gave the town epitomises their dreams. Using a phrase from the book of Hosea, they called it Petach Tikvah, "the Gateway of Hope". Today it is the sixth-largest city in Israel.

A Right Based on History

The Jewish connection with Israel did not begin with Zionism,[1] a word coined in the 1890s. It goes back 4,000 years to the first recorded syllables of Jewish time, God's command to Abraham: "Leave your land, your birthplace and your father's house and go to the land that I will show you" (Genesis 12:1). Seven times God promised Abraham the land, and repeated that promise to Isaac and Jacob. If any nation on earth has a

1. Political movement founded as an official organization in 1897 by Theodor Herzl for the return of the Jewish people to their homeland and the establishment of a Jewish state in Palestine.

right to any land—a right based on history, attachment, long association—then the Jewish people has a right to Israel.

Judaism—twice as old as Christianity, three times as old as Islam—was the call to Abraham's descendants to create a society of freedom, justice and compassion under the sovereignty of God. A society involves a land, a home, somewhere where the "children of Israel" form the majority, and can thus create a culture, an economy and a political system in accordance with their values. That land was and is Israel.

Jews never left Israel voluntarily. They never relinquished their rights. They returned whenever they could: in the days of Moses, then again after the Babylonian exile, then again in generation after generation. [Spanish philosopher and Hebrew poet] Judah Halevi went there in the 12th century. So did [medieval Jewish philosopher and Torah scholar] Maimonides and his family, though they found it impossible to stay, [Spanish Talmudist and physician] Nachmanides went after being exiled from Spain. There was a large community there in the 16th century. There are places, especially in Galilee, where they never left at all.

An Unjust Denial of Rights

Those with a sense of history long ago recognised the injustice of denying Jews their ancestral home. In 1799, Napoleon, at the start of his Middle East campaign, called on Jews to return (the campaign failed before there was a chance to act on this proposal). So did many British thinkers in the 19th century, among them Lord Palmerston, Lord Shaftesbury, and the writer George Eliot in her novel *Daniel Deronda*.

The Balfour Declaration in 1917, ratified in 1922 by the League of Nations, was an attempt to rectify the single most sustained crime against humanity: the denial of Jewry's right to its land and its subsequent unparalleled history of suffering.

[British prime minister during World War II] Winston Churchill never wavered from this view. There were Arab leaders who understood this too. In 1919, King Faisal [of Saudi Arabia] wrote to the American-Jewish judge Felix Frankfurter: "We Arabs, especially the educated among us, look with the deepest sympathy on the Zionist movement . . . The Jewish movement is national and not imperialist. Our movement [Arab nationalism] is national and not imperialist . . . Indeed, I think that neither can be a real success without the other."

The Right to Self-Determination

The idea that Jews came to Israel as outsiders or imperialists is among the most perverse of modern myths. They were the land's original inhabitants: they have the same relationship to the land as native Americans to America, aborigines to Australia, and Maoris to New Zealand. They were ousted by imperialists. They are the only rulers of the land in the past 3,000 years who neither sought nor created an empire.

In fact, no other people, no other power, has ever created an independent state there. When it was not a Jewish state, Israel was merely an administrative unit of empires: the Babylonians, Persians, Greeks, Romans, Byzantines, Umayyads, Fatimids, Abbasids, Crusaders, Mamluks and Ottomans. The existence of Israel, in ancient times and today, is a sustained protest against empires and imperialism: against the Mesopotamia of Abraham's day and the Egyptians of the exodus.

Do we really need a Jewish state? Yes. There must be some place on Earth where Jews can defend themselves, where they have a home in the sense given by the poet Robert Frost as "the place where, when you have to go there, they have to take you in". Every nation has the right to rule itself and create a society and culture in accordance with its own values. That right, to national self-determination is among the most basic in politics. Today there are 82 Christian nations and 56 Muslim ones, but only one Jewish one: in a country smaller than

An Achievement of Jewish History

The very identity of Palestine as a unit of human society is an achievement of Jewish history. The country lost its separate character with the Jewish dispersion and only assumed a specific role in history when the Palestine mandate was ratified. The mandate acknowledged this history by setting Palestine in a distinct and separate context in relation to the Arab world. "I am persuaded," declared President [Woodrow] Wilson on March 3, 1919, "that the Allied nations with the fullest concurrence of our own Government and people are agreed that in Palestine shall be laid the foundation of a Jewish Commonwealth."

Abba Hillel Silver, Vital Speeches of the Day,
October 15, 1947.

the Kruger National Park [in South Africa], one quarter of one per cent of the land mass of the Arab world.

Arab Refusal of Jewish Offers for Partition

Long ago, Jews recognised the right of the Arab population of the land to a place of their own. There were various plans for the partition of the land into two states, one Jewish, one Arab, in the 1920s and 1930s. Jews accepted them; the Arabs rejected them. In 1947, the United Nations voted for partition. Again, Jews accepted, the Arabs refused. [Israeli prime minister] David Ben-Gurion reiterated the call for peace as a central part of Israel's Declaration of Independence in May 1948. Israel's neighbours—Egypt, Jordan, Syria, Lebanon and Iraq—responded by attacking it on all fronts.

The offer was renewed in 1967 after the Six-Day [Arab-Israeli] War. The response of the Arab League, meeting in

Khartoum in September 1967, was the famous "Three Nos": no to peace, no to negotiations, no to the recognition of the State of Israel. The call was repeated many times by [Israeli prime minister] Golda Meir, and always decisively rejected.

The boldest offer was made by [Israeli prime minister] Ehud Barak at Taba in 2001. It offered the Palestinians a state in the whole of Gaza and 97 per cent of the West Bank, with border compensations for the other 3 per cent, with East Jerusalem as its capital. The story is told in detail in Dennis Ross's *The Missing Peace* (Ross was the chief negotiator). Many members of the Palestinian team wanted to accept. The Saudi ambassador at the time, Prince Bandar bin Sultan, said: "If [Palestinian leader Yasser] Arafat does not accept what is available now, it won't be a tragedy, it will be a crime."

Palestinians Betrayed

Tragically, the Palestinians have been betrayed by those who claimed to be their supporters.

They were betrayed in 1948 by the Arab states who promised them that if they left now they would return soon, all Jews having been expelled. They were betrayed by the Arab nations to which they fled, who refused to grant them citizenship, in marked contrast to Israel and its treatment of Jewish refugees from Arab (and other) lands.

They were betrayed by countries that encouraged them to pursue violence instead of peace, bringing poverty to an entire population which, under Israeli rule from 1967 to 1987, had achieved unprecedented levels of affluence and economic growth. They are betrayed today by those who encourage impossible expectations—Palestinian rule over the whole of Israel—thus condemning yet another generation to violence, poverty and despair.

The Egyptians, who ruled Gaza between 1949 and 1967, could have created a Palestinian state, but did not. The Jordanians, who ruled the West Bank during the same years, could have created a Palestinian state, but did not. Instead, Egypt persecuted its Islamist intellectuals, sentencing many to death. The Jordanians expelled the Palestinians in 1971, after killing almost ten thousand of them in 1970 in the massacre known as "Black September". The only country that has ever offered the Palestinians a state is Israel.

Unsuccessful Israeli Efforts for Peace

What has systematically derailed Israel's efforts for peace is the fact that every concession it has made, every withdrawal it has undertaken, has been interpreted by its enemies as a sign of weakness, and has led to more violence, not less. The [1993] Oslo [peace] process led to suicide bombings. Ehud Barak's offer led to the so-called El Aqsa Intifada [Palestinian uprising in 2001]. The withdrawals from Lebanon and Gaza led directly to the onslaught of Katyushas and Kassams [guided missiles]. How does any nation make peace under these conditions? [Palestinian Islamic fundamentalist organization] Hamas and [Islamic political and paramilitary organization] Hizbollah have made it clear that they do not seek peace. They seek Israel's destruction.

Under constant threat of violence or war, Israel's achievements have nonetheless been immense. It has taken a desolate landscape and turned it into a place of farms, forests and fields. It has taken immigrants from more than 100 countries, speaking more than 80 languages, and turned them into a nation. It has created a modern economy with almost no resources other than the creative gifts of its people. It has sustained democracy in a part of the world that had never known it before. It has taken Hebrew, the language of the Bible, and made it speak again. It has taken a people devastated by the Holocaust and made it live again. Israel remains a Petach Tikvah, a gateway of hope.

"Palestinians are the natives of the land that was called Palestine for the last several thousand years until 1948, when Jewish foreigners changed its name to Israel."

Palestine Is the Native Land of the Palestinians

Susan Abulhawa

In the following viewpoint, Susan Abulhawa condemns Israel for violating the rights of Palestinians and claiming their land. Palestinians, she argues, are the true natives of the land—historically, legally, culturally, ethnically, and genetically. According to Abulhawa, Israel has robbed Palestinians of almost everything, treats them as subhuman, and refuses to grant them the same privileges as Jews in their native land.

Susan Abulhawa is a political commentator and the founder and president of Playgrounds for Palestine, a children's organization dedicated to upholding the right to play for Palestinian children.

As you read, consider the following questions:

1. Of what ancient peoples are the Palestinians natural descendents, according to Abulhawa?

Susan Abulhawa, "Our Home and Native Land: Palestine," *Canadian Dimension*, vol. 42, March–April 2008, pp. 28–29. Reproduced by permission of the author.

2. According to the author, what rights are Palestinians being asked to give up?

3. To what does Abulhawa say Israel wants Palestinians to attest by recognizing its right to exist as a Jewish state?

In the 1980s we gave up 78 per cent of our homeland to try to pick up the pieces of our lives on the remaining 22 per cent of Palestine. This was, and remains, the only true (brave or otherwise) concession ever made in the so-called "Middle East Conflict."

A Palestinian Diaspora

Next came [summit meetings at] Camp David, then Madrid, then Oslo, then another Camp David, Taba, Wye, (deep breath) Sharm el-Sheikh, the Disengagement, the Road Map. Through it all, Israel continued to divide, carve out, confiscate and settle that 22 per cent. They scattered us into a diaspora [a people dispersed from its territory], shut down our schools, bombed damn near every inch of the West Bank and Gaza, herded us into ghettos, set up checkpoints all around us and employed every tool of imperialism, times ten, to get rid of us or subjugate us as a cheap labour force.

Then we arrived at yet another surreal meeting in the clouds: Annapolis [site of the 2007 Middle East peace conference]. Everyone was invited except the PLO [Palestine Liberation Organization]—the sole and only legitimate representative of the Palestinian people—and the democratically elected members of the Palestinian Authority (that would be [Palestinian Islamic fundamentalist organization] Hamas). At this meeting, Israel threw us a few bones, like releasing some prisoners (who will most likely get rounded up again when the hype dies down) while it intentionally starves 1.4 million human beings in Gaza, cutting off fuel, electricity and clean drinking water. Annapolis will serve only to move Israel a little closer to stamping out the "refugee problem,"

A Zionist Invasion

The Zionists are conducting an aggressive campaign, in fact, an invasion. For no matter with what apparel it is clothed, religious, humanitarian, or political, the Zionist movement for the possession of Palestine is nothing but an invasion that aims, by force, at securing and dominating a country that is not theirs by birthright.

Jamal el-Husseini, Vital Speeches of the Day,
October 15, 1947.

those Palestinians and their descendants whose homes, farms, property and history Israel stole.

True Natives in All Respects

Palestinians are the natives of the land that was called Palestine for the last several thousand years until 1948, when Jewish foreigners changed its name to Israel. We are the natives in every sense of that word: historically, legally, culturally, ethnically and even genetically! True there were Jewish tribes in that land some 3,000 years ago. There were also Canaanites, Babylonians, Sumerians, Philistines, Assyrians, Persians, Romans, Byzantines and Brits. Palestinians are the natural descendants of all of these peoples who passed through that land, intermarried and converted between religions. When you understand this, it becomes clear why Palestine has always been a multi-cultural, multi-ethnic and multi-religious society. In other words, the idea of "tolerance" and co-existence, which the West fought to attain and claims to cherish and hold dear, was already a reality in Palestine.

Israel has taken that ideal, turned it on its head, and beat it to a pulp so every Jew in the world can have a place where he or she can go and see none but fellow Jews. Remarkably, the world sees nothing wrong or out of the ordinary with this, and would like us simply to live with it and negotiate with a juggernaut military power that has made no secret of its desire and intent to take all of Palestine and get rid of as many of us Gentiles as it possibly can.

The Issue of Human Rights

Never in history has the world so cruelly called upon an oppressed, robbed and battered native people to sit down with their oppressors to "negotiate" for their freedom. Even worse, what we are expected to negotiate away are our basic human rights in order to have a few checkpoints removed so we can rename those ghettos—surrounded by a twenty-foot concrete wall with guard towers—a "state."

We are being asked to give up our natural right to return to the homes from which we were forcibly removed because, and only because, we are not Jewish. We are asked, as native Muslims and Christians, to give up our natural right to live and thrive in Jerusalem as we have for all of time. We are told that we should not expect to have the right to control our own water, economy, airspace, or borders. Why? Why should we accept such an inferior status and inferior fate? We are not children of a lesser god that we should be expected to relinquish. God-given, self-evident rights accorded and upheld for the rest of humanity. We are not animals to be disposed of so that Jewish individuals around the globe can have dual citizenship, a sort of summer country in the Hamptons.

Outrageous Terms of Negotiation

Would anyone have thought to support the desire of White South Africans to live as separate and superior humans and expect Black South Africans to "negotiate" with the Apartheid government for their basic human rights? Of course not! Anyone with a mind and conscience took for granted that Blacks have equal rights as Whites. That is self-evident and non-negotiable. So is our right as non-Jews in Palestine to be accorded the same rights and privileges as Jews in our ancestral homeland. Human dignity and equality simply should not be topics of negotiation in the twenty-first century.

Even more vulgar is Israel's insistence that we recognize its right to be a state of the Jewish people. This country stole everything from us—our homes, our holy places, our trees and farms, our institutions, our history and heritage, the cemeteries where our grandparents and forefathers are buried—because we are not the right kind of human in their eyes. They want us not only to attest that such an affront to humanity is legitimate and appropriate, but that it is somehow a right!

Let me, as one dispossessed and disinherited Palestinian, say with all the force of my love and anguish for my country, my family and my countrymen, that I do NOT recognize such a right. A right is something inherently and unquestionably just. Jewish exclusivity and entitlement at the expense of non-Jews is not a right, for God's sake. It is racism!

> "The Palestinian-Arab citizens [of Israel] are granted an inferior citizenship and face a separate and unequal reality."

Israel Is an Apartheid State

Nimer Sultany

In the following viewpoint, Nimer Sultany argues that Israel is an apartheid, not a democratic, state—Jews and Palestinian-Arabs are not equal citizens. More than half of the Arab families are poor, and the majority of Arab citizens live in the poorest communities, some in villages lacking such basic services as water and electricity, Sultany asserts. The Israelis, Sultany points out, have even built walls to separate Arab and Jewish neighborhoods and Arab and Jewish cities.

Nimer Sultany is a Palestinian citizen of Israel and a doctoral candidate at Harvard Law School.

As you read, consider the following questions:

1. According to Sultany, what percentage of the total population of Israel is Palestinian-Arab?

2. According to the author, what do recent studies reveal about the Arab population of Israel in regard to standard of living, gross domestic product per capita, and level of health?

3. What similarities does Sultany note between South African apartheid and the Arab reality in Israel?

I magine the following situation in the United States:

The US amends the constitution to define itself as a "White Evangelical and democratic state" and leaves "equal protection of the laws" outside the constitution; a federal organ called the White Evangelical National Fund promotes settlement and allocation of land for White Evangelicals only; a federal organ called White Evangelical Agency encourages and helps White Evangelicals all over the world to immigrate to the US since it is the Promised Land for Whites; a federally-funded Center for Demography working to increase the birthrates of White Evangelicals to ensure their status as a majority and discusses ways to "persuade" non-white citizens to have less children; a federal Immigration and Absorption Department dedicated exclusively for White Evangelicals; a law prohibiting mixed marriages inside the US between American citizens and non-White-Evangelical foreigners (the Supreme Court upholds the law since Earl Warren is no longer on the bench); an immigration law providing automatic citizenship and financial government benefits for White Evangelicals only; the administration declares most of the private lands as public domain owned collectively by white people, and non-whites are denied any rights in these lands; the president appoints a Chief Evangelical Priest for the US, the administration funds his office as well as dozens of White Evangelical religious schools and institutions, and the Congress starts its session after the elections by reading Biblical verses; the head of the FBI publicly states that non-white citizens are a "strategic threat" and "demographic threat" to the White Evangelical character of the country; some members of the Congress publicly and routinely demand the expulsion of the non-white citizens; 65% of the white majority regularly expresses in public opinion polls its demand from the administration to encourage the emigration of non-whites outside the country; and 60 years of constant official state of emergency with Emergency Regulations invoked occasionally to prevent non-white leaders from leaving the country and to close their newspapers and NGOs.

Unfortunately this is the daily reality of the Palestinian-Arab citizens in Israel (18% of the total population). All the above-mentioned elements, and more, exist in the Israeli law and political culture: Jewish National Fund, Jewish Agency, etc. Yet, many pro-Israelis defy the facts and still argue that Israel is a democracy where Jews and Arabs have equal rights.

Conversely, Israeli NGOs, international human rights organisations and UN committees regularly expose and protest about the situation of the Palestinian citizens in Israel. The UN committee on economic, social and cultural rights, to mention one example, expressed in 1998 and 2003 its concern that the "excessive emphasis upon the state as a 'Jewish State' encourages discrimination and accords a second-class status to its non-Jewish citizens".

A recent study has revealed that the Human Development Index (a measure for standard of living, poverty, and progress) of the Arab minority in Israel ranks in the 66th place out of 177 countries—very similar to Libya, and 43 slots below the general ranking of Israel, which is 23rd. The GDP per capita for the Arab minority is a third of the GDP per capita of the Jewish majority, and is identical to the GDP per capita of Romania and Iran. The level of health amongst the Arab population is lower than countries like Costa Rica and Cuba.

Various studies have shown that: 60% of the Arab families in Israel are poor; 60% of the poor children in Israel are Arab; 90% of the Arab citizens live in communities ranked in the bottom three clusters of local communities in economic terms;

92% live in separate Arab communities; dozens of Arab villages lack any basic services (water, electricity, sewage, health care, education system, etc), and their homes are constantly threatened by demolition and frequently demolished. These villages are unrecognised by Israeli law in spite of the fact that they had existed long before the law was enacted, or even before the state existed.

Six hundred Jewish communities have been established since 1948, but not a single Arab community; 85% of the Arab citizens' lands have been confiscated since 1948; 96% of the land in Israel is owned by the state, Jewish National Fund and the Jewish Agency. Arab citizens are virtually prohibited from buying, leasing or using these lands.

Sometimes people think that separation walls exist only in the Occupied Palestinian Territories. However, separation walls exist also inside Israel separating between Arab and Jewish citizens. Here are three examples:

In the city of Led between the Arab neighborhood Pardes Shnir and the Jewish Nir Zvi, Sharon's government and Led's local municipality built a wall more than four metres (13 ft) high and 1.5 km long.

In the city of Ramleh between the Arab Jawarish and the Jewish Ganei Dan, there is a wall 4 metres high and 2 km long.

Between the wealthy Jewish city of Caesarea and the poor Arab village of Jisr Az-zarka a dirt mound six metres (20 ft) high and one kilometre long was built by the Jewish city.

Moreover, routinely in places like Ashkelon, Ashdod, Jerusalem, Led, Migdal, Safed, Ramleh, Karmiel, Yerocham, and Rakefet organised groups call for expelling Arab students, workers or residents or blocking them from residing in Jewish cities. Sometimes this is done with the help of the local municipality or the government. The "arguments" are familiar: they corrupt our women, they contaminate our spiritual life, they bring crime and noise, they are unpleasant, and they lower the value of our apartments.

Sometimes it is argued that the analogy to South African apartheid is false since Arab citizens have the right to vote as well as to be elected to the parliament. However, Coloureds and Indians were able to vote in South Africa after the constitutional reforms in 1983, and nobody claimed that this stopped the apartheid from being apartheid. The same goes for Israel.

In sum, the Palestinian-Arab citizens are granted an inferior citizenship and face a separate and unequal reality. Hence the false argument that "Arabs and Jews are equal citizens" amounts to either ignorance or ideological blindness (or both). The fact that most of the Jewish citizens perceive Israel as a democratic state is unsurprising. In fact, this is another similarity between Israel and South Africa under apartheid: the privileged whites argued all the time—until the collapse of the regime—that it was a "democratic" system.

| "No objective observer could claim that
there is Apartheid in Israel."

Israel Is Not an Apartheid State

Robbie Sabel

In the following viewpoint, Robbie Sabel argues that Israel is being falsely accused of being an apartheid state. Arabs take part in the political process, Sabel declares, and racial and religious discrimination are criminal offenses. According to Sabel, the fact that Israel is considered a Jewish state is not evidence of an "apartheid-like" situation, and the intent of the apartheid campaign is to delegitimize the state of Israel.

Robbie Sabel served as legal adviser to the Israeli Ministry of Foreign Affairs from 1985 to 1993 and is a visiting professor of international law at the Hebrew University in Jerusalem.

As you read, consider the following questions:

1. According to Sabel, how did the campaign to try and equate Zionism first with racism and then with apartheid get started?

Robbie Sabel, *The Campaign to Delegitimize Israel with the False Charge of Apartheid.* Baltimore: Jerusalem Center for Public Affairs, 2009. Copyright © Jerusalem Center for Public Affairs. Reproduced by permission.

2. The author contends that "no objective observer could claim that there is apartheid in Israel." What examples of Israeli society and law does he give to support this claim?

3. According to Sabel, what major facts are ignored by those who contend that in occupied territory Israeli law applies to Israeli settlers but not to the local Palestinian population subject to Israeli military administration?

Attempts to smear Israel with the abhorrent phenomenon of racism and Apartheid have reached the level where I believe Israel must react. . . .

If Israel's detractors can somehow, by analogy, associate the Jewish movement for self-determination with the Apartheid South African regime, they will have done lasting and maybe irreparable damage. Analogy to something odious is a very effective tool. It diverts attention from the reality of the subject, in this case Jewish self-determination and Israel, to a regime that is universally detested.

The comparison of Israel to South Africa under white supremist rule has been utterly rejected by those with intimate understanding of the old Apartheid system. . . .

History of Apartheid Campaign

The genesis of the campaign to try and equate Zionism, the Jewish national movement, with racism and consequently Apartheid came from the coalition between the Arab states and the Soviet Union with their allies in the non-aligned movement in the 1970s. They used their automatic majority in the UN General Assembly to pass the 1975 resolution which defined Zionism as a form of racism. This resolution was widely condemned by Christian leaders as anti-Semitic. . . . The resolution was subsequently rescinded by the General Assembly in 1991, . . . but nevertheless the poisonous calumny had been planted.

The UN's World Conference Against Racism, Racial Discrimination, Xenophobia and Related Intolerance, held in Durban, South Africa, in September 2001, gave the Israel Apartheid calumny new force in international circles. The Declaration of the NGOs [nongovernmental organizations] at the Durban meeting openly stated: "We declare Israel as a *racist, Apartheid* state in which Israel's brand of *Apartheid* as a crime against humanity has been characterized by separation and *segregation, dispossession, restricted land access, denationalization, 'bantustanization' and inhumane acts*". . . .

Then in 2006, former President Jimmy Carter published his bestselling book, *Palestine: Peace Not Apartheid.* Although he wrote at the end of his book that the situation in Israel "is unlike that in South Africa," in subsequent public appearances he stressed the comparison between Israel and Apartheid South Africa. Carter chose to use the term "Apartheid" in his title to create controversy. His book gave the defamation of Israel as an Apartheid state new traction. . . .

What Apartheid Really Means

Apartheid has been defined as a "social and political policy of racial segregation and discrimination enforced by white minority governments in South Africa from 1948 to 1994." A dictionary definition is "racial segregation; *specifically*: a former policy of segregation and political and economic discrimination against non-European groups in the Republic of South Africa." It was a situation where the black majority of the population was segregated, discriminated against, and denied the right to vote in the general elections and participate in the government.

Among the prominent features of South African Apartheid policies were:

- Prohibition of marriages between white people and people of other races.

- Prohibition of extra-marital sex relations between white and black people.

- Forced physical separation between races by creating different residential areas for different races.

- Prohibiting a black person from performing any skilled work in urban areas except in those sections designated for black occupation.

- Prohibiting colored persons from voting in general elections.

- Requiring all black persons to carry a special pass, at all times. No black person could leave a rural area for an urban one without a permit from the local authorities.

- Prohibiting strike action by blacks.

- Establishing a Black Education Department. . . . Black students were banned from attending major white universities.

- The so-called "petty segregation" in all public amenities, such as restaurants, swimming pools, and public transport. . . .

The Nature of Israeli Society

Israel suffers from all the internal strains and tensions that every immigrant society endures. The continuous security threats facing Israel add to the tension. The presence of the Arab minority, some of whom have strong family and cultural bonds to their kinsmen in hostile Arab states, is another unsettling factor. However, no objective observer could claim that there is Apartheid in Israel.

Israel is one of the more open societies in the world. Jews comprise some 80 percent of the population, but it is a multiracial and multi-colored society. Israel has universal suffrage with free elections and an independent and effective judiciary. The Arab minority actively participates in the political process. There are Arab parliamentarians, including Arabs as Deputy Speakers of the Knesset [Israeli parliament]. There are Arab judges, including on the Supreme Court, Arab cabinet ministers, Arab heads of hospital departments, Arab university professors, Arab diplomats in the Foreign Service, and very senior Arab police and army officers.

The Law of the Land

Incitement to racism in Israel is a criminal offence. A number of Israeli towns have mixed Arab-Jewish populations. . . . It is a crime under Israeli law for any public body to discriminate on the basis of race or religion. The Israel Supreme Court has ruled that "the rule prohibiting discrimination between persons on grounds of race, sex, national group, community, country of origin, religion, beliefs or social standing is a basic constitutional principle, intertwined and interwoven into our basic legal concepts and forming an integral part of it."

The law prohibiting discrimination in public places has been interpreted broadly by the courts as applying to even private places, including schools, libraries, pools, and stores serving the public. A law from the year 2000 bans any form of discrimination concerning the registration of students by governmental and local authorities or any educational institution. It is not surprising that after examining the false analogy between Israel and Apartheid South Africa, Rhoda Kadalie, a South African anti-Apartheid activist, concludes in an analysis . . . that:

> Israel is not an Apartheid state. . . . Arab citizens of Israel can vote and serve in the Knesset; black South Africans could not vote until 1994. . . . Whereas Apartheid was established through a series of oppressive laws that governed which park benches we could sit on, where we could go to school, which areas we were allowed to live in, and even

whom we could marry, Israel was founded upon a liberal and inclusive Declaration of Independence. . . . Israeli schools, universities and hospitals make no distinction between Jews and Arabs. An Arab citizen who brings a case before an Israeli court will have that case decided on the basis of merit, not ethnicity. That was never the case for blacks under Apartheid.

Thus, it is difficult to visualize a society less akin to South Africa under Apartheid.

Jewish State Does Not Equal Apartheid

Since accusations of actual Apartheid in modern Israel lack credence, the accusation is made that the very fact that Israel is considered a *Jewish* state proves an "Apartheid-like" situation. . . .

The crux of the accusation against Israel is encapsulated in the often-repeated charge that the racism of Israel "is symbolized most clearly in Israel's Jewish flag, anthem and state holidays." The accusers have not a word of criticism against the tens of liberal democratic states that have Christian crosses incorporated in their flags, nor against the Muslim states with the half crescent symbol of Islam. For a Western state, with Jewish and Muslim minorities, to have Christmas as a national holiday is permissible, but for Israel to celebrate Passover as a national holiday is somehow racist. For various Arab states to denote themselves as Arab Republics is not objectionable, but a Jewish state is racism and Apartheid. . . . The Palestinian national movement is legitimate, but the Jewish national movement is Apartheid. . . .

None of the accusations against Zionism as being a form of Apartheid point out that it is perhaps the only national movement that has received explicit support and endorsement both from the League of Nations and from the United Nations. . . . It was the United Nations that in 1947 called for the establishment of "Independent Arab and Jewish States."

Accusation by Metaphor

Israel is the only country in the world that is accused by its enemies of practicing apartheid without racism; of perpetrating a Holocaust without gas chambers; of engaging in genocide without mass murder; of committing war crimes without targeting civilians; and of being the worst human rights violator in the world, while having one of the most responsive legal systems in the world. This is accusation by metaphor, prosecution by propaganda, trial by bigotry, guilt by hyperbole, and sentence by sloganeering. In demeaning these historically contingent and emotionally powerful terms, those enemies of Israel deflect attention away from genuine apartheid regimes, actual practitioners of genocide, real war criminals, and grievous human rights violators.

Alan Dershowitz, The Case Against Israel's Enemies, *2008.*

Here again, presumably, the call for an independent Arab state is legitimate, but the call for an independent Jewish state is somehow racism. . . .

The Peace Process and the Wall

Another track to try and associate Israel with the South African Apartheid regime is to claim that the Middle East Peace Process is somehow a manifestation of Apartheid. . . .

The Peace Process has had its detractors, but it is surely strange to ignore that the process has given hope for a lasting peace settlement. It gained its protagonists three Nobel Peace Prizes and the support, in democratic elections, of the majority of the population of Israel and of the Palestinians in the West Bank. The Israel-Palestinian Oslo Declaration of Principles, as part of the Madrid peace process, was signed as an act of support by the United States and by the Russian Federation. The Interim 1995 Israeli-Palestinian Agreement, also part of the Madrid process, was signed as an act of support by representatives of the United States, the Russian Federation, Egypt, Jordan, the European Union, and Norway. The Middle East "Roadmap," incorporating the Madrid principles, has been repeatedly endorsed by the UN Security Council. The United Nations General Assembly has endorsed these Israeli-Palestinian agreements; they have even been mentioned with approval by the International Court of Justice. This is hardly "Bantustans," puppet regimes that were not supported by a single state other than South Africa which unilaterally created them. The virulent criticism would seem to derive from those who are not interested in any peaceful resolution.

The most popular use of the word "Apartheid" in relation to Israel appears to be in connection with Israel's security fence. The Israeli Army has explained the need for the fence: "Between Israel and the areas of the Palestinian Authority [administrative organization set up to govern parts of the West Bank and Gaza Strip] there is no border or natural obstacles, which, to date, enables the almost unhindered entry of terrorists into Israel. The security fence that exists along the Gaza Strip has proven its defensive robustness and the vast majority of infiltration attempts through it were discovered and thwarted."

Those criticizing the construction tend to use the word "wall" and call it a separation wall though in fact "only a tiny fraction of the total length of the barrier (less than 3 percent or about 10 miles) is actually a thirty-foot-high concrete wall." Any border fence in fact serves to separate areas and one may hope for a world with no borders. However, as long as Israel has to face terrorist acts, it is legitimate for it, as it is for other states, to erect a barrier to prevent terrorist attacks and illegal crossings. Those calling the fence the "Apartheid wall" make frequent reference to the advisory opinion of the International

Court of Justice on the issue. They fail to point out that in its opinion on the wall the International Court of Justice at no time made any analogy or reference to Apartheid or referred to an "Apartheid wall." Furthermore, although the International Court criticized the route of the "wall" as being beyond the 1949 "Green" Armistice Line, the court was careful not to deny Israel's right in principle to build such a security fence.

The "Occupied Territories" and Settlements

Some exponents of the "Israel Apartheid" thesis, aware that they have a problem with branding Israeli society as an Apartheid society, limit themselves to claiming that the Israeli administration and Israeli settlements in the West Bank are a manifestation of Apartheid.

Exponents of the Israel-Apartheid campaign claim that eastern Jerusalem is subject to an Apartheid regime and argue that "Since the illegal annexation by Israel in 1967, all successive Israeli governments have made great efforts to reduce significantly the number of Palestinians residing in eastern Jerusalem, to assure Israeli sovereignty, [and] a Jewish majority." This is a very strange accusation. The Arab population of Jerusalem was 68,000 in 1967, comprising 25 percent of the total population. In 2007 the Arab population of Jerusalem was 260,000, comprising 35 percent of the total population of the city.

The existence of some roads in the West Bank where, for security reasons, Israeli and Palestinian traffic is separated is also presented as proof of Apartheid. This claim completely ignores the very real security threat to Israeli road traffic and incidentally also ignores the fact that "Israeli traffic" includes the vehicles of the more than one million Arabs who are Israeli citizens, and who also have been subject to terrorist attacks.

No Israeli Jurisdiction

A major theme of the "Israel applies Apartheid to the territories" campaign is that Israeli law, with all its built-in safeguards of individual rights, applies to Israeli settlers but not to the local Palestinian population who are subject to Israeli military administration. Such criticism ignores two major facts. The first is that since 1993, as part of the peace process, it is the Palestinian Authority that has jurisdiction over the overwhelming majority of Palestinians in the West Bank. [Palestinian Islamic fundamentalist organization] Hamas, which splintered off from the Palestinian Authority, has jurisdiction over the whole population of the Gaza Strip. The vast majority of Palestinians in the West Bank and Gaza are hence subject neither to the Israeli military administration nor to regular Israeli law. Their laws, courts, police, prisons, taxes, etc., are Palestinian and Israel has no jurisdiction over them. . . .

The other issue the criticism ignores is that any attempt to apply internal Israeli law to the few local Palestinians who are still under temporary Israeli military administration would be met by vehement world opposition. According to international law, temporary military administration is the norm to be applied to territories that are not under the sovereignty of a state. . . .

The issue of settlements in the West Bank is a matter of debate in the international community as well as within Israeli society. . . . The issue is one of boundaries between Israel and a future Palestinian state. It is not an Apartheid system of a minority controlling a majority, but a border dispute that hopefully will be negotiated peacefully in the near future.

The Goal Behind the Apartheid Campaign

The Apartheid campaign against Israel has another revealing feature. It rarely deals with the massive abuse of human rights or cases of real Apartheid elsewhere in the world. In other words, it singles out Israel with a false accusation. . . . The campaign against Israel is not based on a concern with the universal application of human rights, but on something else. This treatment of Israel is nothing less than an effort to delegitimize the Jewish state, by attributing to it the most heinous crimes. . . .

Perhaps the most chilling indication of the real purpose behind the "Israel is Apartheid" campaign is revealed in one of the most active websites behind the campaign. They write that among the goals of "prosecution for the crime of Apartheid is to force Israel to—

> Enable the true majority to return to power over their own lands, while protecting the rights of ethnic minorities."

In other words, the real goal behind the Apartheid campaign is the denial of the legitimacy of the State of Israel and the determination that the only status the Jewish population in Israel can hope for is that of a "protected" ethnic minority in an Arab Palestinian state.

> "International law grants the right to leave or return to one's country only to individuals, not as a collective right as the Palestinians claim."

There Is No Right of Return

Richard L. Cravatts

In the following viewpoint, Richard L. Cravatts contends that the right of return has no legal or diplomatic standing. Those declaring otherwise, he maintains, are misreading the United Nations resolutions on purpose to gain their own ends. Palestinians were not "victimized" by the creation of Israel, according to Cravatts. He asserts that the creation of Israel did not wipe out or dispossess a Palestinian nation—the concept of a Palestinian national identity did not crop up until the 1960s.

Richard L. Cravatts is director of Boston University's Program in Publishing at the Center for Professional Education.

As you read, consider the following questions:

1. On what thinking is the Palestinian propaganda campaign for the "right of return" based, according to Cravatts?

2. According to the author, how have the Palestinians and their Arab enablers prolonged the myth of victimhood?

3. According to law professor Ruth Lapidoth, as cited by Cravatts, why does UN Resolution 194 not support the Palestinian claim for an unqualified right of return?

When President [George W.] Bush hosted the Annapolis [Middle East peace] conference in 2007, Israel, the Palestinians, and U.S. Secretary of State Condoleezza Rice left hoping that some resolution to the decades-old conflict would reveal itself by the end of 2008. The likelihood of such an outcome by the end of Bush's presidency [2009] seems to be steadily evaporating, as Israel's [prime minister] Ehud Olmert exits office in disgrace, and Palestinian chairman Mahmoud Abbas, though softening his rhetoric, is still adamant that "Palestinian refugees must have the right to return to their homeland," as he . . . asserted in his meeting with [President] Hosni Mubarak of Egypt, and that "Jerusalem and the right of return are inalienable Palestinian rights, too."

Stumbling Block to Peace

For its part, [Palestinian Islamic fundamentalist organization] Hamas, Abbas' political foe, was even more direct and stringent on this issue, contending that any negotiation "which disregards the basic rights of the Palestinians, and their internationally-guaranteed Right of Return will not be accepted by the Palestinian people."

All sentient observers of the Palestinian issue know that the "right of return" issue is a core tactic in rendering real peace, any viable Arab/Israeli solution, effectively impossible, that the prospect of some four or five million Palestinian refugees flooding into what is now Israel would, as University of Haifa professor Steven Plaut puts it, "derail Israel demographically and turn it into the Rwanda of the Levant."

The demand for a right of return, a notion referred to by Abbas and his Palestinian supporters as "sacred" and an "enshrined" universal human right granted by UN resolutions and international law, in fact has no legal or diplomatic standing at all, and is part of the propaganda campaign that is based on the thinking that if Israel cannot be eradicated by the Arabs through a military war, it can be effectively destroyed by forcing it to commit demographic suicide.

The Myth of Victimization

In the first place, the concept of the right of return uses as its core notion that the Palestinians were "victimized" by the creation of Israel, that they were expelled from a land of "Palestine" where they were the indigenous people "from time immemorial," as historian Joan Peters put it in her book of the same name. The recounting of this wistful reading of history has enabled the Palestinian cause to become the obsession of the Leftist West, Middle East Study Centers on university campuses, the United Nations, and throughout the Arab world where Jew hatred helps fuel a central, persistent myth of Zionist oppression of fellow Muslim brethren.

More importantly, far from being either a "sacred" or, for that matter, legal right, the right of return is a one-sided concoction that deliberately misreads United Nations resolutions for political advantage, and conveniently embraces only those portions that fit the intent of Arabs to make good on their long-standing intent to "drive Israel into the sea." In continually repeating the lie that they are victims of the "Zionist regime" and that they were expelled from a country of their own and condemned to unending refugee status, the Palestinians—and their Arab enablers—have prolonged the myth of victimhood. But as Professor Efraim Karsh, head of Mediterranean Studies at King's College at the University of London, and the author of *Fabricating Israeli History: The New Historians*, points out, "this claim of premeditated dispossession is itself not only baseless, but the inverse of the truth. Far from being the hapless victims of a predatory Zionist assault, the Palestinians were themselves the aggressors in the 1948–49

No Unlimited Right of Return

You cannot expect Israel to acknowledge an unlimited right of return to present day Israel, and at the same time, to give up Gaza and the West Bank and have the settlement blocks as compact as possible, because of where a lot of these refugees came from. We cannot expect Israel to make a decision that would threaten the very foundations of the state of Israel, and would undermine the whole logic of peace.

Bill Clinton, "Remarks by the President at the Israel Policy Forum Gala," US Embassy-Israel, January 8, 2001.

war, and it was they who attempted, albeit unsuccessfully, to 'cleanse' a neighbouring ethnic community. Had the Palestinians and the Arab world accepted the United Nations resolution of November 29, 1947, calling for the establishment of two states in Palestine, and not sought to subvert it by force of arms, there would have been no refugee problem in the first place."

Thus, the accusations that the creation of the State of Israel led to the eradication and dispossession of a Palestinian 'nation,' and that Israel continues to obstruct and deny the Palestinians' right of self-determination, are spurious at best, since, as Robert Spencer, scholar of Islamic history, notes, before the 1967 war when Israel took control of Gaza and the West Bank, no one—including the Palestinians themselves—thought of themselves as a nation, that this "supposed national identity was invented in the 1960s in what turned about to be an extraordinarily successful ploy to adjust the paradigm of the Arab-Israeli conflict with the newly-minted Palestinians as the underdogs."

UN Resolution 194

Nor was the land that the Palestinian Arabs fled from in what would become Israel ever land to which Palestinian refugees could ever make a legally sound claim. "None of the West Bank and Gaza Strip has ever been 'Palestinian Land,'" says columnist and historian David Meir-Levi. "Before Israel's, the last legal sovereignty over these territories was that of the Ottoman Empire. The British Mandate was a temporary caretaker control established by the League of Nations. And from 1948 to 1967, the West Bank was illegally occupied and annexed by Jordan, and the Gaza Strip by Egypt—both in stark defiance of international law, the Fourth Geneva Convention, and UN resolutions 181 and 194."

There is some irony in the fact that the Palestinians have repeatedly violated both the spirit and intent of 194, that particular UN resolution containing a reference to the concept of 'return' to one's country, although two key points are characteristically ignored by those now pointing to this source as justification for their legal claim. First, Resolution 194 was the product of the UN General Assembly and "is an expression of sentiment and carries no binding force whatsoever," meaning that it is meant to make recommendations but not binding law. What it did suggest, however, was that "the refugees wishing to return to their homes and live at peace with their neighbors should be permitted to do so at the earliest practicable date, and that compensation should be paid for the property of those choosing not to return and for loss of or damage to property which . . . should be made good by the Governments or authorities responsible."

According to the evaluation of law professor Ruth Lapidoth of The Hebrew University of Jerusalem, this language precludes an interpretation of the UN resolution that supports a Palestinian claim for an unqualified right of return as opposed to a suggested one. "Though the Arab states originally rejected the resolution," she wrote (specifically because it would mean giving implicit recognition of the existence of Israel), "they later relied on it heavily and have considered it as recognition of a wholesale right of repatriation."

Resolution Also Applies to Jewish Refugees

But according to Professor Lapidoth, "this interpretation . . . does not seem warranted: the paragraph does not recognize any 'right,' but recommends that the refugees 'should' be 'permitted' to return. Moreover, that permission is subject to two conditions—that the refugee wishes to return, and that he wishes to live at peace with his neighbors," something the Arab world, even now, has clearly never seen fit to do. And there is another significant aspect of the "refugee" problem from the 1940s that everyone demanding rights of return and reparations for Palestinian refugees conveniently forgets: some 800,000–900,000 Jews, some of whom had lived in Arab lands for 2000 years and were fully integrated into those societies, were expelled and all their wealth (estimated to be about ten times that of the Palestinians, estimated to be $100 billion) confiscated as the nascent Israel was being established.

So for observers like Professor Karsh, the recommendations of Resolution 194 "could as readily apply to the hundreds of thousands of Jews who were then being driven from Arab states in revenge for the situation in Palestine," and in fact were meant to, since the refugees mentioned in the resolution are purposely not defined as being either Arab or Jew. In fact, many diplomats and officials had anticipated an exchange of refugees, as has happened successfully in other similar social upheavals, where Palestinian refugees would have been absorbed in Arab states and Jewish refugees would have settled in Israel—exactly what happened to some 600,000 Jewish refugees from Arab lands.

Legal scholars also point out that international law grants the right to leave or return to one's country only to individuals, not as a collective right as the Palestinians claim. More importantly, no population of refugees has ever presumed that the right of return—if such a right even exists—could be claimed, not only by the original refugees, but also by all of their descendants.

The Arab States and the Refugee Problem

Also, the Arab world has never agreed to assimilate Palestinians into their respective countries and solve the refugee problem; instead, the blame for the plight of the dispossessed Palestinians has been assigned singularly to Israel. "Among the dozens of countries to which tens of millions of refugees have fled for asylum," says Joseph E. Katz, a Middle Eastern political and religious history analyst, "the only instance in which the 'host countries refused,' as a bloc, to assist properly, or even to accept aid in the permanent rehabilitation of their refugees, occurred in the 'Arab states,'" violating the thinking of the resolution itself which foresaw "reintegration of the refugees into the economic life of the Near East, either by repatriation or resettlement."

No one would have imagined that, of the roughly 100,000,000 refugees created by international conflicts just since World War II, only the Palestinians would not have been resettled in the million and a half square miles of Arab land; instead, they have been made to tragically languish by their Arab brethren who still hypocritically demand their right to return only to the tiny 8000 square-mile piece of land that is now Israel.

The Real Motivation

So it is significant that people who should know better, including Mr. Abbas, continue to promiscuously refer to the right of return as a clear, legally-binding right with which Israel has repeatedly interfered. But the motivation is clear: prolong the myth of Palestinian victimization and grant them, as part of that mythology, exclusive international recognition and supposed legal rights. Why? "Unlike all those many millions of other people considered refugees in the late 1940s," answers Professor Plaut, "the 'Palestinians' were the only ones for whom the 'right of return' to their previous homes was considered an entitlement. The reason was not a selective affection for Palestinians, but a selective hostility towards Israel and Jews."

If Palestinians could embrace the notion of a secure life in a Palestinian state that already exists, Jordan, and stop sacrificing themselves on the myth of a return to a homeland that was never and can never be exclusively their own, they may be able to live, finally, in peace with their Israeli neighbors who seek the same safety and self-determination themselves.

> "The implementation of [Palestinian
> refugees'] inalienable rights [to return]
> is the key to a permanent peace."

Israel Must Implement the Right of Return

Salman Abu Sitta

In the following viewpoint, Salman Abu Sitta argues that Palestinian refugees must return to their homeland to bring an end to their sufferings. He maintains that they have the right to return because, according to international law, the mass denationalization of people is illegal if the place they live undergoes a change of sovereignty. The refugee problem must be resolved, Abu Sitta asserts, for there to be permanent peace.

Salman Abu Sitta is author of several works on Palestine, the founder and president of the Palestine Land Society, a member of the Palestine National Council, and general coordinator of the Right of Return Congress.

As you read, consider the following questions:

1. According to Abu Sitta, where do the majority of Palestinian refugees live?

2. According to the author, why should Palestinian refugees return home?

3. According to Abu Sitta, what is the real reason for Israel's racist practices?

One of the most important lessons we have learned from the 60-year Palestinian-Israeli conflict is that the essence of the struggle has not changed: It is the expulsion of the people of Palestine from their homes and the confiscation of their land. Since then the Palestinian refugees have been dispersed all over the world, many of them living in deplorable conditions in exile, others suffering under occupation or virtual siege, harassed by friend and foe alike. The implementation of their inalienable rights is the key to a permanent peace. All else, including a Palestinian state, so-called regional cooperation or other contrived devices to obscure this fundamental issue, is peripheral. . . . The refugees issue is still the main problem to contend with and is imposing itself on every agenda of negotiating the question of Palestine. . . .

Resettlement Plans

Today, the majority of the refugees live in Palestine and environs. According to the United Nations Relief and Works Agency (UNRWA), at the end of June 2005, 4,283,892 Palestinian refugees were registered with UNRWA. Approximately 41.9%, or 1,795,326, were registered in Jordan: 22.6%, or 969,588, in the Gaza Strip; 16.1%, or 690,988, in the West Bank: 10%, or 426,919 in the Syrian Arab Republic; and 9.4%, or 401,071, in Lebanon. Of the registered refugees, 30.3%, or 1.3 million, lived in 58 UNRWA camps. Many refugees are still not registered. . . . Thus, the total number of refugees is 6,322,000 (2005), but 88% of all Palestinians are still living in Palestine and in surrounding countries.

The proximity of the refugees and their unquenched desire to return home explains the feverish Israeli attempts to bring in as many immigrants as possible from such diverse places as Ethiopia and Russia, just to fill the depopulated Palestinian areas. It is not surprising therefore that over four dozen schemes proposed and promoted vigorously since 1948 to dispose of the refugees anywhere in the world, except their homes, have utterly failed.

Why Should the Refugees Return?

First, it is perfectly legal in accordance with international law. The well-known UN General Assembly Resolution 194 has been affirmed by the international community 135 times in the period 1948–2000. There is nothing like it in UN history. This universal consensus elevates the weight of this resolution from a "recommendation" to an expression of the determined will of the international community. International law also prohibits mass denationalization of a people if the territory in which they live undergoes a change of sovereignty. Thus, the refugees are entitled to return to the homes they lost and to a restoration of their nationality as well. The Right of Return is supported by the Universal Declaration of Human Rights and the many regional conventions based on human rights law. It is also derived from the sanctity of private ownership, which is not diminished by change of sovereignty, occupation or passage of time.

Second, the Right of Return is sacred to all Palestinians; they have no intention of abandoning it. Third, there is no acceptable reason why they should not return. None of the Israeli claims to the contrary withstands serious scrutiny.

The Demographic Case

It is often claimed that there is no room in Israel for the refugees' return. In fact, this is not true. Previous studies on the subject can be summarized as follows:

It is possible to divide Israel's 46 natural regions (before re-division) into three groups: Group A, 1,628 square kilometers, has a Jewish population of just over 3 million (67% of Israel's total Jewish population). This area is, roughly, the land acquired by Jews during the period of the British Mandate. Most Jewish settlement after the creation of the state centered around this initial area.

Group B, 1,508 square kilometer, is almost the same size but not in the same location as the land owned by the Palestinians who remained in Israel after the 1948 war. (Since 1948, Israel has confiscated two-thirds of the property of its Palestinian citizens). In this area, there are 436,000 Jews, or 9.6% of all the Jews in Israel, along with 92,000 of Israel's Palestinian citizens. Thus, 77% of Jews live in 15% of Israel's territory.

That leaves Group C, 17,381 square kilometers, located in two large blocks, corresponding roughly to the Northern and Southern Districts as per Palestine and Israel's administrative divisions. This is the land and heritage of about 6 million refugees who were expelled from their homes in 1948 and their descendants. About 1 million Jews live in Group C, but 80% of them live either in cities that were originally Palestinian, many of which are now mixed, or in a number of small new "development towns."

This leaves 200,000 rural Jews who exploit vast areas of refugee land—the largest part of the remainder of the land is used for military purposes and afforestation. Most of these rural Jews (160,000) are residents of the *moshavim* (cooperative farms) and *kibbutzim* (collective farms). Today only 8,600 *kibbutzniks* live on agriculture. Thus, the rights of 6 million refugees are pitted against the prejudices of 8,600 *kibbutzniks*. . . .

Restoration of Palestinian Villages

Another Israeli claim is that all traces of villages are lost and have been built over by housing for new immigrants. This claim, again, is false.

All the existing built-up areas in Israel today have been plotted, and we superimposed on them the sites of 530 Palestinian towns and villages depopulated in 1948. The striking result is that the sites of an absolute majority of such villages are still vacant. All village sites, except one each in the subdistricts of Safed, Acre, Tiberias and Nazareth, are vacant. Naturally, the area most affected is the coastal strip, especially in the Tel Aviv suburbs. There, a dozen village sites have been built over as a result of the expansion of the city. The displaced refugees from these built-over areas now number 110,000, or only 3% of all registered refugees. A number of village sites west of Jerusalem, and north and south of Tel Aviv, have been built over.

However, well over 90% of the refugees could return to empty sites. Of the small number of affected village sites, 75% are located on land totally owned by Arabs and 25% on Palestinian land in which Jews have a share. Only 27% of the villages affected by new Israeli construction have a present population of more than 10,000. The rest are much smaller. . . .

What Is the Cost-Benefit Account?

If a historical conflict is solved by the return of 6 million refugees to their homes in accordance with international law, what is the price of this huge achievement?

The 160,000 residents of *moshavim* and *kibbutzim* who would be affected may decide to stay and rent land from the Palestinian owners, or they may decide to relocate. As for the *kibbutzim*, today less than 3% of Israelis live on *kibbutzim*, most of which are near bankruptcy. . . .

The economic return of these vast resources is meager and diminishing. In addition, a major change in government policy affecting *kibbutzim* and *moshavim* land has taken place in the last 10 years. This policy in effect transferred the Israel Land Administration (ILA)-controlled land into private and industrial ownership, including permitting the rezoning of residential construction to accommodate Russian immigrants or to

A More Constructive Role

There are already one million Palestinians living in Israel as citizens. Some Israeli Jews see them as a kind of "fifth column." But many Israelis recognize that, despite second-class status, political and economic exclusion and Israel's conflict with their brethren, Palestinian citizens of Israel have been loyal and productive citizens. How much more constructive would their role be if their countrymen and women in exile were accorded the same right to return that Israel gives to Jews anywhere in the world? Surely, returning refugees could be equally productive members of the same society.

Ali Abunimah and Hussein Ibish, American-Arab
Anti-Discrimination Committee, 2001. www.adc.org.

build commercial outlets, shopping malls and private apartments. The *kibbutzim*, according to this change, would be compensated for this transaction at 51% of its value. This made the bankrupt farmers very rich overnight, allowing them to pocket the value of (Palestinian) land they never owned in the first place. . . .

Ariel Sharon, the former prime minister, was quoted as saying, "The only way to absorb the immigrants was by taking land from the Kibbutz. . . . I knew the [economic] hardship they are experiencing . . . it is better they build on the land and sell houses."

Thus, the return of 6 million refugees and the end of the historical conflict is weighed against the livelihoods of 8,600 *kibbutzim*, an economically bankrupt movement now mostly abandoned by the Israelis themselves.

Water and Agriculture

Water can be a cause of war in the Middle East. It has been widely reported that Israel's invasion of the West Bank and Syria in 1967 was designed to control the headwaters of the Jordan River and its tributaries and aquifers of the West Bank.... Each of these resources, diverted from Syrian and West Bank waters, amounts to 500 million cubic meters per year, much of which is wasted. Since 1948, two-thirds of Israel's consumption of 2,000 million cubic meters per year is stolen from Arab sources....

[One study] recommends that the wasted water could be "sold" to Jordan and the West Bank in a peace deal. Apart from the irony that Israel would be selling illegally confiscated water back to its rightful owners, the fact is that Israel's enormous water and land resources are exploited by so few to produce so little. If this land and water were turned over to the lawful owners, there would be little loss to Israel ... and tremendous gain in peace prospects....

The "Jewish Character" Syndrome

The claim that the "Jewish character" of Israel would be threatened is repeatedly cited to justify the denial of the fundamental right of Palestinians to their land and property. But what is the meaning of "Jewish character"? If it entails policies that deny the return of refugees and allow unlimited numbers of Jewish immigrants in their place, this is best described by [authors W. Thomas Mallison and Sally V.] Mallison as "a euphemism for the Zionist discriminatory statutes of the state of Israel which violate the human rights provisions of the Partition Resolution.... The United Nations is under no more of a legal obligation to maintain Zionism in Israel than it is to maintain apartheid in the Republic of South Africa." ... In 1998 the UN treaty-based Committee on Economic, Social and Cultural Rights said that Israel's "excessive emphasis upon the State as a 'Jewish State' encourages discrimination and accords a second-class status to its non-Jewish citizens." Israel cannot maintain this position for long. The moral and legal weight of human rights will catch up with it one day.

All the facts concerning this concept indicate that the notion of the numerical superiority of Jews is a cruel time game in which the refugees rot in their camps until the Israelis realize, or admit, that this contention is a horrible hoax, intended to keep the conquered land empty until its owners give up or are gotten rid of by a "final solution" to the Palestinian problem.

If the "Jewish character" refers to religious practice, this has rarely been a problem in the Arab and Islamic world. Numerous historians have demonstrated that Islamic and Arab societies have treated Jewish minorities far better than Christian European societies.

There is no ethical or legal justification for the maintenance of a "Jewish character" that denies human rights or violates international law. The real reason for Israel's racist practices is to maintain its hold on Palestinian land and keep it as a reserve for future Jewish immigration. . . .

Israel Must Change Its Policies

Both Israelis and Palestinians agree that there can be no peace without a resolution of the refugee problem, but they differ on the method of resolution. Israelis believe that they can extend and legalize their original ethnic cleansing operation. This is an illusion. The fact that all of their so-called "resettlement schemes" have been nipped in the bud by governments and people alike is proof enough of that.

The Israelis have no legal, ethical, practical, demographic or economic reason to persist in denying the refugees' rights. Israel's position is solely derived from racist policies, and as the only one left in the world to deny Palestinian refugees' rights, is condemned by the rest of the world.

It is a matter of conjecture to estimate how many Israeli Jews would wish to live in a non-racist democratic country. Nor does anyone know how many would leave for fear of indictment of war crimes and crimes against humanity. But this is a fruitless exercise, since the principle of "universal jurisdiction" would chase them anywhere.

The price Israel has to pay for permanent peace is far less than imagined. In a land that is relatively underpopulated today in most parts, in which half its citizens are, on average, outside the country at any given time and where the appetite of its young people for war has waned considerably, peace—especially a peace that guarantees the rights of Jews and Palestinians under international law—should be highly desirable. All Israel has to do is become a truly democratic country for all its citizens and interpret its Law of Return[1] to mean "right of return" on a legal, not a racist, basis. In its absorption capacity, it should give priority to those who are lawfully qualified to return, not those who bring seeds of conflict and war. Priority should be given to those who own, not those who conquer.

---

1. Legislation enacted in Israel in 1950 that grants a right of immigration to Israel and automatic citizenship to any Jew from anywhere.

Periodical Bibliography

The following articles have been selected to supplement the diverse views presented in this chapter.

Khalid Amayreh   "Abu Mazen: Don't Mess with the Right of Return," *Sabbah Report*, September 15, 2008. www.sabbah.biz/mt/.

Gary A. Anderson   "Does the Promise Still Hold? Israel and the Land," *Christian Century*, January 13, 2009.

Warren Goldstein   "This Is Apartheid?" *Jerusalem Post*, August 12, 2008.

Ami Isseroff   "The Mythical Peace That Is just Out of Reach," ZioNation: Zionism and Israel Web Log, November 29, 2009. www.zionism-israel.com.

Isabel Kershner   "Premier Says Some Settlements Will Always Be Israel's," *New York Times*, January 25, 2010.

Yisrael Medad   "There Can Be Nothing Illegal About a Jew Living Where Judaism Was Born," *Los Angeles Times*, June 28, 2009.

David M. Phillips   "The Illegal-Settlements Myth," *Commentary*, December 2009.

Steven Plaut   "Out with the Occupiers!" *Jewish Tribune*, November 4, 2009.

Benjamin Pogrund   "Catastrophic, but Not Apartheid," *Haaretz*, May 4, 2008. www.haaretz.com.

CHAPTER 3

Is Peace Possible
Between Israel
and the Palestinians?

Chapter Preface

Peace has been elusive in the Middle East for many years. Since 1948, there have been civil wars in Jordan and Lebanon, and wars between Iraq and Kuwait and Iraq and Iran, to name a few. While these conflicts have been devastating for all involved, none has endured as long or has had as many ramifications as the wars, altercations, and animosity between the Israelis and the Palestinians. For them, conflict has become a way of life even in peacetime, and war looms as a constant threat.

Much time, money, and effort has been expended in attempts to bring compromise, reconciliation, and peace to the Middle East in general and to the Israelis and Palestinians in particular. Summits dedicated to finding ways to bring resolution to the conflict have been held off and on for decades. Mediators from the United Nations, the United States, the European Union, and Russia, among others, have proposed peace plans, negotiations, and solutions. So have the Arabs and the Israelis. In 1993, there were the Oslo Accords, agreed upon by Israel and the Palestine Liberation Organization (PLO), the group originally established by the Arab League in 1964 to deal directly with the problem of the Palestinian Arabs. In 2001 came the Taba talks between Israel and the Palestinian Authority, and in 2003, the Road Map for Peace plan put forth by the United States, the European Union, Russia, and the United Nations. In 2007, two plans originally proposed in 2002—the Elon Peace Plan and the Arab Peace Initiative—were revived. The original Elon Peace Plan proposed relocating Arabs from the West Bank and other areas to Jordan; the 2007 version proposes that the Palestinians become citizens of Jordan and residents of Israel. The Arab Peace Initiative offers Israel full peace, recognition, and normalization of relations in exchange for the establishment of a Palestinian state in the

West Bank and Gaza with its capital in East Jerusalem and a "just" settlement of the Palestinian refugee crisis. None of these, however, has brought the peace desired.

Some inroads have been made over the years. In 1979, Egypt became the first Arab country to make peace with Israel, which many consider a groundbreaking diplomatic achievement that profoundly affected the Middle East. In 1993, the PLO signed an agreement recognizing Israel's right to exist. The following year, Jordan became the second Arab state to sign a peace treaty with Israel.

Nonetheless, no plan yet has achieved the goal to end the Israeli-Palestinian conflict. Some people believe that no plan will work until Arabs and Israelis each change their mindset about all the land belonging to them exclusively. Others believe that no plan will work as long as a conservative hardliner heads the Israeli government or Arab terrorists desire to put Israel out of existence. Still others believe that the conflict is a generational one that has been going on for centuries and that any plan, no matter what solutions or how logical a peace process are proposed, will succeed in bringing the peace most Israelis and Palestinians profess to want.

The viewpoints in this chapter demonstrate the depth and complexity of the issues involved in the pursuit for peace between the Israelis and Palestinians. Only time will tell whether the compromises needed for a peaceful solution can be achieved. Meanwhile, most Israelis and Palestinians probably would agree with Professor Moshe Sharon of Jerusalem's Hebrew University that "in the present situation in the Middle East and in the foreseeable future 'Peace' is nothing more than an empty word."

> "Only a genuine, interpersonal policy of
> reconciliation can instigate real peace
> in the Middle East and lay the founda-
> tion for eternal peace between Jews and
> Arabs."

Peace Is Possible Between Israel and the Palestinians

Hubertus Hoffmann

In the following viewpoint, Hubertus Hoffmann contends that in order to have a workable and lasting peace for Palestine and Israel a dual strategy of power and reconciliation must be put into practice. According to Hoffmann, Palestine must establish a new, credible democratic political party headed by a new and vital leader. He asserts that Israel must make reconciliation an integral part of its peace policy.

Hoffmann is a German entrepreneur, geostrategist, and president and founder of the World Security Network Foundation, the largest global elite network for foreign and security policy.

As you read, consider the following questions:

1. According to Hoffmann, what is the top priority for everyone who really wants peace in Palestine and for Israel?

2. According to Hoffmann, what fundamental strategic mistake is being made by Israel, the Palestine Authority, Saudi Arabia, other Arab states, the European Union, and the United States relative to their peace plans and policies?

3. According to the author, what steps must the Sunni Arab states, the European Union, and the United States take to help bring about a real and lasting peace?

For everyone who really wants peace in Palestine and for Israel, the top priority is to establish a forward-looking and credible new political democratic party for Palestine ("Change Palestine! Movement"), headed by a new [U.S. president Barack] Obama-style leader.

After presenting his program of change, he should first become Prime Minister, integrating new faces into the administration, and later winning the trust of the Palestine people with a rolling consensus. He may then be elected President and a true and respected majority leader of Palestine.

Portrait of a New Palestinian Leader

Not [Palestinian Islamic fundamentalist organization] Hamas, nor [Palestinian political and military organization opposed to Israel] Fatah: something new for the young frustrated majority.

Not a puppet of the U.S. nor Israel but a local leader supported at first by several Arab countries like Saudi Arabia, Jordan, Egypt, and the UAE [United Arab Emirates], and by the EU [European Union].

For this historic movement we need an independent Palestinian personality from outside, ideally a successful business leader who as a Palestinian patriot dedicates his life to this historic task. He must not be burned out by political struggles of the past, nor corrupt. He should be young, credible, eloquent, and courageous, should have political skills, and should work well with the media. A man of great character and soul, sharing the vision for a better democratic future for Palestine. No radical and no puppet, but a man of vision and wisdom. . . .

A New, Credible Political Party Essential

Until now the Palestinian people have only had the choice between bad and worse—not bad and better—as there is no credible party to vote for. This must change. . . .

Without such a new political party for Palestine every peace plan will fall apart like dust in the wind or melt away like snow in the sun. Any treaty will not be worth the paper signed. . . .

Fatah cannot be reformed any more and will never get back its lost credibility. This rotten movement will not survive more than several weeks if its unofficial support by Israel . . . in the West Bank is withdrawn after a peace treaty. Its leadership has lost credibility and is seen as too corrupt and too close to Israel and the U.S. . . .

Hamas may talk softer now for mere tactical reasons but in core and spirit it will always remain a totalitarian movement in Iranian fashion, dependent on its long-time relationship to that Shia [Islamic] regime and its brothers in Lebanon, the Hezbollah [Shia terrorist organization]. You cannot reform Hamas into a soft democratic movement. . . .

Palestine needs a new credible force and a fascinating new personality to lead this young people to freedom, wealth and reconciliation with Israel. The Change Palestine! Movement should integrate several personalities from Fatah and Hamas and also imprisoned fighters but be able to keep full control of the armed forces, law and order and foreign affairs. It should become a catalyst of unity. It should learn from the great thinkers of the world like Albert Einstein, who preached that you cannot solve a problem on the level of thinking where you have created it, or the wisdom of [American writer and philosopher] Eric Hoffer who told that a war (of the Palestine people) is only won after you have turned your enemy (Israel) into your friend. It should establish a Palestine Truth and Reconciliation Commission . . . to start healing the wounds of the past and looking for reconciliation inside Palestine and with the people of Israel as well.

A New, Double Strategy

Another fundamental strategic mistake of Israel, the Palestine Authority [administrative organization that governs part of the West Bank and Gaza Strip], Saudi Arabia, other Arab states, the EU and the US is that their peace plans and policies are focused on treaties and land for peace and do not implement an overall double strategy of power and reconciliation, hawk and dove. Exactly that is needed.

The Codes of Tolerance Project of the World Security Network Foundation . . . digs deep into the foundations of peacemaking. It shows that with power and military means alone peace can not [be] preserved. It enforces a new double strategy of power and reconciliation, soft and hard factors which are needed yet too often neglected. . . .

The so-called 'soft factors' are not soft but hard realities of peacemaking. Contrary to the beliefs of some security leaders, it is naive to think and plan war and peace in areas like the Middle East without them.

If you have no strategy, funding and promotion of the extremely important soft factors, and if you do not win the hearts and minds of the population, you must lose.

Need for Reconciliation in Israeli Policy

Israel's 60-year-old bunker mentality means it believes that security can be produced with military means and by destroying the military capabilities of its enemies. It is missing the core of peacemaking, to separate the overwhelming majority of the peace-loving Palestinians from the few radicals and to turn the Palestine people into friends and partners of Israel. This must become a serious aim of any credible Israeli security policy and a second pillar as important as the military means. This includes treating the Palestinians as partners in peace and not as enemies; not as second class citizens but as equals . . .

Israel's policy toward its neighbours is lacking, perhaps fatally so, the common element in successful peace politics: reconciliation.

Israel needs, in the interests of its own survival, a new peace policy consisting of the "Uzi [submachine gun] and the olive branch": a credible double strategy of reconciliation on the one hand, and deterrence through both military operations against terror organizations and conventional and nuclear weapons on the other.

The historical formula for Israel's survival, surrounded as it is by hostile countries and the threat of state-sponsored terrorism, is the "hawk plus dove". The hawk alone does not bring peace. The invasions in Lebanon in 2006 and in Gaza [in 2009] have proven this again.

Israel Needs a New Peace Policy

In the next one hundred years, Israel will only be able to survive in its historic location, surrounded by a numerically superior enemy rich with petrodollars, if it places reconciliation with its Arab neighbours as *conditio sine qua non* [non-negotiable condition] of a genuine Israeli peace policy, and supports reconciliation with just as much energy, imagination, patience, and money as the necessary but insufficient military operations against terrorists. Israel needs a reconciliation offensive to supplement the necessary traditional military and power politics.

Only a genuine, interpersonal policy of reconciliation can instigate real peace in the Middle East and lay the foundation for eternal peace between Jews and Arabs, who already live well together in Israel.

Active power politics, be it the targeted killing of terrorists or the invasion of Gaza, only bring about a limited tactical advantage for several months, and not a lasting peace.

Power politics is the necessary complement to peace politics. Alone, however, it is insufficient for security and peace.

In other words, Israel needs a new peace policy, which is credible externally. . . .

To this end, Israel can draw on European "best practices". There, millions of people were driven from their homelands following [World War II], including twelve million Germans in the East. . . . They were peacefully integrated into their new country and made lasting peace in Europe possible through reconciliation and the renunciation of violence and a return home. . . .

A Fresh Approach for Palestine

Palestine needs a fresh approach for peace as well. Needed is not only a new leader but a new elite. Palestine needs a new, younger leadership elite and dynamic personalities who take over political responsibilities.

This new elite must put forward a new, progressive design for a free Palestine. They should develop a counter-concept to the totalitarianism of the supposed Islamic dictators à la Hamas, who are not concerned with peace and the mercifulness of the Prophet, but rather naked power for themselves. Otherwise, Palestine will sink further into an orgy of violence and murder.

The Palestinians should make their way toward a modern, tolerant society with the help of a Marshall plan[1] sponsored by Saudi Arabia, the Gulf States, the U.S., and the EU.

With suicide attacks and a few rockets from Gaza you can never defeat the Israel Defense Forces. Even threats from

1. Economic aid program enacted by the United States to help rebuild Europe after World War II.

Tehran, including nuclear strikes, are not credible because Israel has more than enough nuclear weapons to destroy Iran several times over. Nuclear deterrence works and will work in the future well.

The Road to Peace

The Sunni Arab states, the EU and the new Obama administration must impeach the radicals in Palestine and Israel and establish a new political movement of change and progress and a double strategy of power and reconciliation. Only from this solid foundation can any peaceful solution for this troubled region work. Only after the forming of such a base can a real chance for a real peace plan and treaty arrive. . . .

This is not a utopia. . . .

We know it can be done. . . .

We believe this is the only way to solve the problem at its root and to bring peace to the people of Palestine and Israel.

"After a decade of Hamas arming itself within a Palestinian state that narrows Israel to eight miles wide—Hamas re starts the war against a country it re mains pledged to eradicate."

Hamas Does Not Want Peace with Israel

Charles Krauthammer

In the following viewpoint, Charles Krauthammer contends that the peace plan put on the table by the Palestinian fundamentalist organization Hamas offers not a long-term peace but merely a ten-year truce. He maintains that it is in effect a phony peace and that Israel is smart not to accept it at face value. According to Krauthammer, past Palestinian experience has taught Hamas how to manipulate the situation for the short term so that it can achieve its goal of eradicating Israel in the long term.

Charles Krauthammer is an American Pulitzer Prize–winning syndicated columnist and political commentator whose weekly column appears in the Washington Post.

As you read, consider the following questions:

1. According to Krauthammer, what is Hamas offering Israel?

Charles Krauthammer, "The Hamas 'Peace' Gambit," *Washington Post*, May 8, 2009, p. A-27. Reproduced by permission of the author.

2. What actions has the Obama administration taken that the author says Hamas sees as an opportunity?

3. According to Krauthammer, what is Hamas leader Khaled Meshal's gambit?

"Apart from the time restriction (a truce that lapses after 10 years) and the refusal to accept Israel's existence, Mr. Meshal's terms approximate the Arab League peace plan. . . ."

—*Hamas peace plan, as explained by the* New York Times

"Apart from that, Mrs. Lincoln, how did you enjoy the play?"

—*Tom Lehrer, satirist*

The [*New York*] *Times* conducted a five-hour interview with [Palestinian Islamic fundamentalist organization] Hamas leader Khaled Meshal at his Damascus [Syria] head-quarters. *Mirabile dictu* [wonderful to say], they're offering a peace plan with a two-state solution. Except. The offer is not a peace but a truce that expires after 10 years. Meaning that after Israel has fatally weakened itself by settling millions of hostile Arab refugees in its midst, and after a decade of Hamas arming itself within a Palestinian state that narrows Israel to eight miles wide—Hamas restarts the war against a country it remains pledged to eradicate.

There is a phrase for such a peace: the peace of the grave.

Hamas's Political Strategy

Westerners may be stupid, but Hamas is not. It sees the new American administration [of Barack Obama] making over-tures to Iran and Syria. It sees Europe, led by Britain, begin-ning to accept [Shiite terrorist organization] Hezbollah. It sees itself as next in line. And it knows what to do. [Former Palestine Liberation Organization leader] Yasser Arafat wrote the playbook.

With the 1993 Oslo accords, he showed what can be achieved with a fake peace treaty with Israel—universal diplo-

A Palestinian State in Place of Israel

Hamas was created to fight and win holy wars—not to seek peace and sing kumbaya with infidels. Hamas wants a Palestinian state in place of Israel—not next door to Israel. And for Hamas, preventing Palestinian carnage is not a priority. That's not a slander, it's a fact. As Hamas parliamentarian Fathi Hamad eloquently phrased it: "We desire death as you desire life."

Clifford D. May, National Review, *January 5, 2009.*

matic recognition, billions of dollars of aid, and control of Gaza and the West Bank, which Arafat turned into an armed camp. In return for a signature, he created in the Palestinian territories the capacity to carry on the war against Israel that the Arab states had begun in 1948 but had given up after the bloody hell of the 1973 Yom Kippur War.

An Opening for Hamas

Meshal sees the opportunity. Not only is the Obama administration reaching out to its erstwhile enemies in the region, but it begins its term by wagging an angry finger at Israel over the [Israeli prime minister Benjamin] Netanyahu government's ostensible refusal to accept a two-state solution.

Of all the phony fights to pick with Israel. No Israeli government would turn down a two-state solution in which the Palestinians accepted territorial compromise and genuine peace with a Jewish state. (And any government that did would be voted out in a day.) Netanyahu's own defense minister, Ehud Barak, offered precisely such a deal in 2000. He even offered to divide Jerusalem and expel every Jew from every settlement remaining in the new Palestine.

The Palestinian response (for those who have forgotten) was: No. And no counteroffer. Instead, nine weeks later, Arafat unleashed a savage terror war that killed 1,000 Israelis.

The Israeli View

Netanyahu is reluctant to agree to a Palestinian state before he knows what kind of state it will be. That elementary prudence should be shared by anyone who's been sentient the last three years. The Palestinians already have a state, an independent territory with not an Israeli settler or soldier living on it. It's called Gaza. And what is it? A terror base, Islamist in nature, Iranian-allied, militant and aggressive, that has fired more than 10,000 rockets and mortar rounds at Israeli civilians.

If this is what a West Bank state is going to be, it would be madness for Israel or America or Jordan or Egypt or any other moderate Arab country to accept such a two-state solution. Which is why Netanyahu insists that the Palestinian Authority [administrative organization that governs parts of the West Bank and Gaza Strip] first build institutions—social, economic and military—to anchor a state that could actually carry out its responsibilities to keep the peace.

The Two-State Solution: A Palestinian Ploy

Apart from being reasonable, Netanyahu's two-state skepticism is beside the point. His predecessor, Ehud Olmert, worshiped at the shrine of a two-state solution. He made endless offers of a two-state peace to the Palestinian Authority—and got nowhere.

Why? Because the Palestinians—going back to the U.N. partition resolution of 1947—have never accepted the idea of living side by side with a Jewish state. Those like Palestinian President Mahmoud Abbas, who might want to entertain such a solution, have no authority to do it. And those like Hamas's Meshal, who have authority, have no intention of ever doing it.

Meshal's gambit to dress up perpetual war as a two-state peace is yet another iteration of the Palestinian rejectionist tragedy. In its previous incarnation, Arafat lulled Israel and the [Bill] Clinton administration with talk of peace while he methodically prepared his people for war.

Arafat waited seven years to tear up his phony peace. Meshal's innovation? Ten—then blood.

> "Israel is not interested in serious compromises in order to reach a peace agreement which will solve the historical conflict between Israel and the Arabs."

Israel Is Not Ready for Peace

Ziad Khalil Abu Zayyad

In the following viewpoint, Ziad Khalil Abu Zayyad argues that Palestinians are ready and willing to compromise to achieve peace, but Israel is not. He asserts that statements made and actions taken by Islamic fundamentalist organization Hamas, Palestinian leaders, and the Arab world in general prove their willingness to come to an agreement with the Israelis. According to Abu Zayyad, the fixation on security, military force, and fear of attack, however, causes the Israelis to ignore Arab overtures and not support any kind of compromise.

Ziad Abu Zayyad, a Palestinian Arab living in East Jerusalem, is an international relations and English literature student at the Hebrew University of Jerusalem.

As you read, consider the following questions:

1. What three examples does Abu Zayyad give to support his contention that Israelis are not ready to pay the price for what they want?

2. According to the author, what is the Israeli response to Arab statements and actions showing that they are ready to compromise for peace?

3. According to Abu Zayyad, what has made Israel "far away from reaching peace"?

The [December 2009] prisoner's exchange which is being negotiated between Israel and the Palestinians became an interest for both sides. The Israeli rightist government found itself in a place where it cannot decide whether to make the deal or not. Prime Minister [Benjamin] Netanyahu is known for his statements [about] the importance of not negotiating with what Israel considers "terrorist" groups. At the same time Prime Minister Netanyahu finds himself under the pressure of the Israeli public opinion who demands . . . the release of the imprisoned Israeli soldier Gilad Shalit.[1]

Israeli Opposition to a Prisoner Exchange

The principles which Prime Minister Netanyahu and his extreme right government believe in make the situation difficult since any agreement to release Palestinian prisoners will be contradicting with their beliefs. [Palestinian Islamic fundamentalist organization] Hamas says that their demand to release the Palestinian prisoners is legitimate since the Palestinian prisoners are prisoners of war and freedom. On the other hand Israel considers the Palestinian prisoners as terrorists who must stay in prison in order [to] protect Israel's security.

The refusal to release the Palestinian prisoners can be found also in the Israeli left side. The moderate and left

1. Gilad Shalit is an Israel Defense Forces soldier who, at age 19, was captured on June 25, 2006, by Palestinian militants, who continue to hold him.

Israelis believe that any kind of exchange of prisoners between Israel and Hamas will make the situation become worse since Hamas will gain the credit in the Palestinian street.

The real problem in the Israeli position is not about who will gain the credit or how to assure that the security of the Israeli state will not be affected. The problem is that the Israeli leadership and street are not ready to pay the price for what they want. Israel wants peace but does not want to withdraw from the occupied territories. Israel wants Gilad Shalit to come back home but it is not ready to release Palestinian prisoners in exchange. Israel wants security but does not want to admit the right of the Palestinians to live in a state of their own. Although this is the situation, Israeli leaders continue to say that the Palestinians are not ready to become independent and do not want to compromise in order to reach a peace agreement.

Unacceptable Israeli Solutions

The Israeli and some of the West media stated in the past that Israeli leaders such as [Minister of Defense] Ehud Barak and former Prime Minister Ehud Olmert offered the Palestinians good solutions but the problem was that the Palestinians were not ready to sacrifice. Olmert's offer was published a couple of days ago in *Yadeoot Ahronot* Israeli newspaper. The picture of the map which explains the kind of solution which Olmert offered speaks for itself. The Palestinian territories were marked in red and appear on the map as two small areas in the whole historical map of Palestine. A safe way connects between these two areas. Israeli settlements such as Maaleh Adumim are supposed to be kept under an Israeli control. Sources such as Water are to be kept under the Israeli authority. The whole offer which the world talked about does not give the Palestinians twenty percent of what they are asking for.

Then once there is a Palestinian refusal of agreeing on an Israeli offer, the world accuses them of being not ready to sac-

Natural Growth of Settlements: Not a Point of Compromise

Israel's determination to resist meaningful compromises is apparent in the way it confronted the [Barack] Obama administration over the "natural growth" of settlements. Israel maintains that people who are born in a settlement in the occupied territories should be allowed to live there when they grow up, and that the settlements should be allowed to expand "naturally" to accommodate them. It is an absurd argument: research suggests that "natural growth" includes significant numbers of incomers with no previous connections to the settlements. And besides, it does not address the existence of the settlements themselves. Yet it has served Israel's purpose: "It has provided a smokescreen behind which Israel can pursue more significant and urgent construction that, when completed, will truly render the occupation irreversible," says Jeff Halper of the Israeli Committee Against House Demolitions.

Edward Platt, New Statesman, *November 12, 2009.*

rifice for the sake of peace. Most of the Palestinians stated frankly that they are ready to live in peace with Israel if the latter is ready to share the land and respect the idea of a Palestinian independent existence in the area. When [the 1993] Oslo agreement was signed, the Israeli leadership knew what the Palestinians are asking for. Jerusalem, the Palestinian refugees, the prisoners, and the 1967 occupied lands were supposed to be negotiated in order to reach an agreement. Today Israel considers Jerusalem the united capital of Israel, the refugees case as something which cannot be negotiated, the west bank and Gaza as a part of Eretz Israel [the historical land of

Israel] which is in other words the lands of Israel that every Jew has the right to live in. . . . Israeli settlements became legitimate and the peace project turned into Israeli economic offers to hush the Palestinians. . . .

Security: The Israeli Excuse

It is clear that Israel is not interested in serious compromises in order to reach a peace agreement which will solve the historical conflict between Israel and the Arabs. The problem is not in Hamas or the Palestinian leadership or the Arab world who all stated and acted in different ways which proved that they are ready to compromise. . . . So what is the Israeli response? More ideologies which are built on the use of force, army and wars in order to assure the security of the Israeli state and a continuous ignor[ing] of the Arab offers.

Israelis are taught through the different institutions of the state and the community that Israel is always in danger of being attacked by its neighbors. The people are affected by such ideas and therefore it becomes harder to convince them to support any kind of compromise for the sake of reaching a peace agreement with Arabs.

The latest war on Gaza is a good example; the Israeli leadership before the war wanted to prepare the Israeli people for war by convincing them that the war must happen and that the Israeli army is the best regarding the respect of human rights and laws of war. The result was a complete censor on the Israeli media and misleading information which differed from what was really happening in the time of war. More than 1300 Palestinians were killed while many Israelis believed that only tens were citizens and the rest were fighters. The effect of the war resulted in bringing an extreme right government which is useless and caused damage for the picture of Israel in the world. The reason is that the current government states and acts according to the real beliefs of the Israeli state regarding the conflict with the Palestinians without acting and with a lack of skill in directing the conflict.

Israeli Distortion of Islam

Another example are the academic associations; in one of the lectures which studies Radical Islam at the Hebrew University this semester, the lecturer describes Israel as a reason which makes the Islamic world remember how strong it was and how much is needed in order to return the Islamic control over the area. Although the course is supposed to study Radical Islam movements such as Al-Qaida [the terrorist organization responsible for the September 11, 2001, attacks] and other Islamic extrem[ist] movements, it attacks and criticizes the Islamic community since the days of Prophet Muhammad and the whole idea of spiritual belief by claiming that an academic research is not built on spiritualities.

The tens of Israeli students who attend such courses and are supposed to become diplomats and future leaders of Israel are taught about the "danger" and past of the Islamic world and are taught about the extreme side of it with a wider coverage while the change and improvement which are taking place in it are ignored.

In the past Israel used to be proud of its democratic society which gives everyone who lives in it a chance to demonstrate, think, and shout about what he or she believes. Today Israeli peace activists and Palestinian residents of occupied Jerusalem and the West Bank are treated in ways worse than South Africa. The obsession of security made the Israeli security institutions and intelligence service become obsessed of controlling everyone and sometimes preventing an idea from spreading or a group of people from dancing or demonstrating. This illusion made Israel become far away from reaching peace because peace which is obtained by force and security theories will always be in danger of war.

> "I say to my Palestinian colleagues: Do not bemoan the establishment of the State of Israel; establish your own state, rejoice in its establishment and we will rejoice with you."

Peace Is Likely with a Two-State Solution

Tzipi Livni

In the following viewpoint, Tzipi Livni contends that the time has come to put the past aside and make the changes required for peace. The fairest way to resolve the national conflict between Jews and Arabs, Israelis and Palestinians, Livni maintains, is to agree to partition—to have one Jewish state—Israel—and one Arab state—Palestine. She asserts that Arab agreement to partition is the first step on the road to peace.

Tzipi Livni was the Israeli vice prime minister and minister of foreign affairs at the time this speech was given.

As you read, consider the following questions:

1. What does Livni consider a just resolution for the conflict between the Israelis and Palestinians?

2. According to the author, knowing that the Arab-Israeli conflict has a solution is not enough. On what does she believe reaching the solution depends?

3. What more does peace mean than an agreement in exchange for land, according to Livni?

Sixty years ago this week [November 27, 2007], the United Nations passed a resolution to partition the strip of land between the Mediterranean and the Jordan River—the place known to us as the Land of Israel and to others as Palestine. The strip of land where I was born, where my forefathers lived for thousands of years. The strip of land to which the Jewish people yearned to return when in exile, when they prayed for Jerusalem, and to which they returned over the course of hundreds of years. The strip of land where my Palestinian colleagues were born.

I did not come here today to argue about rights. I did not come here to argue whose claims are more justified. I came today to tell my colleagues from the Arab world that the right thing to do is not to relinquish our sense of justice or our belief in rights. I have no intention of asking another nation to do that, just as I do not ask that of myself—and I believe in the Jewish nation's right to all of the Land of Israel. This is the time to think about a different right—the right of our children to live in peace and mutual dignity, according to the values that I believe are the legacy of all the peoples in the region, and certainly the values of all the religions. Your important participation here, even though for some of you this was not an easy decision, testifies to that fact and instills in me hope for the future.

Two States for Two Peoples

True, there is a national conflict between us, whose just resolution is to give expression to the national aspirations of each of the nations in its own state. This is exactly the principle determined 60 years ago, after years of bloodshed between the residents of this country—the principle of two states for two peoples: one—a Jewish state, as decreed by the UN resolution, and the other—an Arab state.

Yes, ladies and gentlemen, the decision to establish the State of Israel alongside an Arab state was meant to provide a response to the past conflict; it is not what created the present conflict. The decision did not determine who was more in the right, but rather what would lead to a life of peace between the peoples.

Even before the State of Israel was established, the Jewish public accepted the principle of the partition of Israel. We chose already then not to resolve the question of rights over the Land of Israel, or the question of historical justice. We decided to embark on a new life in a new state—even if only on part of the territory.

This choice, which was rejected at that time by the Arab world, is still a choice that can be made by the Arab world in general and the Palestinians in particular.

Peace and a Shared Future

On the day that the State of Israel was established, May 14, 1948, our Independence Day, the day that you, my Arab colleagues, call the "Nakba"—the disaster, Israel proclaimed in its Declaration of Independence: "We extend our hand to all neighboring states and their peoples in an offer of peace and good neighborliness, and appeal to them to establish bonds of cooperation and mutual help . . ."

Our hands are still outstretched in peace to the entire Arab and Muslim world without exception, including the Palestinians, Lebanon, Syria, Saudi Arabia, Oman, Bahrain, Morocco and Indonesia.

I am proud at where Israel is today. I am sorry that the Arab world rejected the principle of partition in the past, and I hope and pray that today there is an understanding that

The Most Likely Outcome

By 2033, two states, Israel and Palestine, will be living side-by-side in an uneasy peace, with the risk of war between them and terrorism across their common border diminishing year by year. This two-state solution will not be imposed by the United States or the Arab world. It will be freely chosen by the Israelis and Palestinians themselves. The growing Palestinian majority living between the Mediterranean and the Jordan River will continue to insist on nothing less. And a solid majority of Israelis will by then have come to see a two-state partition of Palestine as essential to Israel's survival as a tolerable place to live and raise their families.

That is not the only outcome possible for 2033. But it is the most likely—and it is the most attractive one for Israelis, Palestinians and the outside world.

David C. Unger, World Policy Journal, *Fall 2008.*

instead of fighting, the right thing to do is to build a shared future in two separate states: one—the State of Israel, which was established as a Jewish state, a national home for the Jewish people; and the other—Palestine—which will be established to give a full and complete solution to Palestinians wherever they may be. Those who are in Gaza and the West Bank, and those in the refugee camps in other Arab countries with temporary status, waiting for a sense of belonging to a national state—the same feeling of wholeness that the establishment of the State of Israel gave to the Jewish refugees who were forced to leave Arab countries and Europe and became partners in building Israel.

A Mutually Beneficial Solution

I believe that the solution of two nation states serves the interests of both sides. Not every celebration of ours is cause for sorrow on the other side, and vice versa. I say to my Palestinian colleagues: Do not bemoan the establishment of the State of Israel; establish your own state, rejoice in its establishment and we will rejoice with you, since for us the establishment of the Palestinian state is not our Nakba, or disaster—provided that upon its establishment the word "Nakba" be deleted from the Arabic lexicon in referring to Israel.

Knowing that the conflict has a solution is not enough. Reaching the solution depends first of all upon us—on the two sides themselves and their ability to conduct negotiations, to touch on the most sensitive points and to provide answers based on the understanding that neither side can obtain everything it wants and that compromises are necessary on both sides.

The solution also depends on the ability of the leaders to cope with extremists and terrorism, and we are not speaking here only of the leaders of the sides directly involved in the conflict. This is the central task of the entire world leadership, and especially of the Arab and Muslim world. . . .

A Need to Unite and Fight for Peace

This is the time for decision. Everyone must decide which side they are on, and the sides, ladies and gentlemen, have changed. They are no longer Israel on one side and the Palestinians on the other side. They are no longer the Arabs on one side and the Jews on the other side.

In one camp is everyone who is sitting here in this room— Jews, Muslims and Christians, Israelis, and Arabs, Americans, and Europeans.

You know who did not come—those who are working against the conference. The states that did not come are those that support terrorist organizations and radical elements in your home countries; those who wish to cause instability in the region. The organizations and leaders who use God's name to sow hatred, to send children out to be killed ... the God we see as the God of mercy and peace.

This is the battle that must be won.

Sitting on the fence will not accomplish it. Neither is one-time participation in an event sufficient. The common goal is comprehensive peace in the region for all the peoples and all the states. Peace is not merely an agreement in exchange for land; peace means ending incitement, ending support of terrorism and actively opposing it, ending arms smuggling, and dismantling terrorist bases of operations. . . .

The Road to Normalization

I have heard those who say that Israel needs to pay for normalization. Such talk is based on an approach whereby normalization is a kind of prize that should be given to Israel only after comprehensive peace is achieved between Israel and its neighbors, an approach that assumes that it is in Israel's interest to achieve normalization with the Arab world instead of a difficult peace process including compromises.

This, ladies and gentlemen, is a mistake.

I admit that Israel wants to live a life of peace and partnership and to establish normal relations with the entire Arab world. Israel's strong desire to make peace with its various neighbors does not replace the process of direct negotiation with the Palestinians, even at the cost of the compromises that will be required of us. . . . The yearning, the goal and the vision that we seek to fulfill—peace with the Palestinians and with our other neighbors—this is the prize. We want to do it.

Agreement and Compromise

Our dream is not to stall for time, and stagnation is not our policy. It does not serve the interests of either side. We are not trying to establish facts on the ground through settlements and we are willing to pay a heavy price in terms of territory for peace. We do not want to control the Palestinians or to dictate their lives. We do not want our children, as soldiers, to stand at checkpoints and screen civilians, and we do not want your children's childhood pictures to be our children, as soldiers, putting their parents through a security check. We have no hidden agenda. Not so long ago, we decided on disengagement. We left Gaza, we dismantled settlements, we withdrew our army, we took risks with the understanding that Gaza will not be the last step.

We want to take the next steps through agreement.

It is clear to us that in order to carry out change, we will have to give up parts of Israel. Our border is the border of security. We are prepared to do so, provided that it does not endanger the lives of our citizens. That is also our obligation towards them.

Normalization is not something that you give and Israel receives; it is something from which everyone benefits. . . .

A Vision of Peace

The world is watching events here in Annapolis [the site of the 2007 Middle East peace conference]. I was pleased with your decision to come here. The picture emerging from here is one of a vision of peace shared by those who are prepared to make the necessary change—and it is a picture worth more than a thousand words. Your presence here is important, not just for the leaders with whom we are meeting today. Your presence is important to the entire world—it is important for you at home, it is important for the Palestinian Authority [administrative unit that governs part of the West Bank and Gaza] and it is important for Israel.

Today's picture is the start of the journey toward peace. . . .

We have paid a heavy price over the years of the conflict. Families have lost their loved ones and we are powerless to soothe the pain of a bereaved mother. We cannot turn the wheel of history back, bring our dead back to life, restore the maimed to health, and return people to their homes. We cannot change decisions that we have made. There is no point in regretting decisions that we could have made in time and missed the opportunity. We can make decisions that will affect the future, and the journey to peace in the region begins once again here, today, in Annapolis.

| "The two-state solution demands of Israel the kind of concessions history wrests from nations defeated at war."

Peace Is Unlikely with a Two-State Solution

Bernard Chazelle

In the following viewpoint, Bernard Chazelle argues that a two-state solution is not realistic from an Israeli perspective because Israel would have to make many tangible concessions for which they would receive only intangible ones in return. According to Chazelle, the Palestinians would take over land, while all Israel would get is promises of peace, secure borders, and recognition of its existence—all of which could be taken back in an instant. The Israelis hesitate to give up so much for what may turn out to be unreliable promises, he maintains.

Bernard Chazelle is the Eugene Higgins Professor of Computer Science at Princeton University.

As you read, consider the following questions:

1. According to Chazelle, instead of being the realistic road to peace it once was, what is the two-state solution now?

2. According to the author, what are the four strategic reasons incremental approaches to the two-state solution have failed so far and two disincentives that have kept Israel from playing along?

3. According to Chazelle, what would Israel have to do if it agreed to a two-state solution to achieve peace?

The Israeli-Palestinian conflict is often narrated as a morality play, where offers are generous, lessons are taught, consciousness is seared, terrorism is rewarded, etc. Let's quit the blame game and focus, instead, on what's feasible and what's not. . . .

What about a one-state solution? Within 10 years, Jews will be a clear minority in the population west of the Jordan, so a democratic unitary state (eg, modeled on South Africa) would mean the end of Israel as a Jewish state, an outcome not everyone would greet with cartwheels. Though rarely discussed, a federal alternative could be envisaged. Besides the sticky issue of land division, however, the physical laws of politics work against it. Absent a modicum of trust and a desire to share a common fate, centrifugal forces might prove too powerful to forestall an eventual breakup. If Belgium, a model of harmony by Mideast standards, can barely pull it off, what chance does a (con)federal "Isratine" have? Don't expect a democratic binational state any time soon.

The Challenge of the Two-State Solution

The two-state solution has its appeal. It would satisfy a majority of Palestinians and confer upon Israel the statehood legitimacy that it craves. It would bring the Jewish state peace with the Arab world along the lines of the 2002 Saudi Initiative, as well as a recognized right of self-defense against Palestinian cross-border attacks. Unfortunately, 40 years of history have gamed the system against the two-state solution. Once the only realistic road to peace, it is now a challenge likely beyond Israel's ability. . . .

With its popularity fading rapidly, the main asset of the two-state solution is its [undisputed] delineation: Taba [the peace summit of] [2001] or any [1967]-border variant that ensures the viability of a Palestinian state. Opponents cite the failure of the 2005 Gaza evacuation to bring peace to the [Gaza] Strip as Exhibit A. They conveniently forget that the occupation continued and the total number of settlers was actually *higher* after the withdrawal than before. They ask, How do we keep a two-state solution from turning into a Qassam [rocket] launch-pad expansion program? Such concerns must and can be addressed. But the stumbling block lies elsewhere—specifically, in a game-theoretic deadlock.

The Issue of Settlement Expansion

To understand this, it is best to begin with a paradox. Everybody knows that to "rewind to '67" would be a risky move for any Israeli leader and that the risk increases with every settlement expansion.... The never-say-die E1 [Israeli settlement] project threatens to cut off East Jerusalem from the West Bank and divide a future Palestinian state into 3 (and arguably 4) [separate] parts. As I drove recently by the giant settlement of Ma'ale Adumim, I wondered how a Palestinian capital could ever be wrested from that urban octopus of Israeli control now girding East Jerusalem. [US secretary of state] Condoleezza Rice's ... bit of cheerleading was promptly acknowledged by an Israeli Cabinet decision to build hundreds of housing units in Givat Ze'ev. The number of checkpoints and obstacles was supposed to go down after [the 2007] Annapolis [peace talks]: it went up by 51. Can Israel be serious about a two-state solution?

When someone embarks on a diet and then proceeds to double his food intake, it is reasonable to wonder if he doesn't secretly enjoy the extra weight. Reasonable, yes; but, in this case, wrong. The crux of the paradox is not that Israel enjoys the status quo but that it has no incentive to play a land-for-peace game *incrementally*. Three reasons for this: Israeli aims are *intangible* (eg, promise of peace) but Palestinian objectives are concrete (eg, land handover); settler withdrawal is *irreversible*, whereas a lull in violence can be broken at any time; finally, the two-state solution is an *asynchronous* trade, ie, an exchange of a present good (land) for a future one (peace). Instead of addressing these deal breakers head-on, ... [US president George W. Bush's 2002] Road Map [for Peace] tossed in a goodie bag full of sops (eg, governance reform, trade offices, demonstration of good faith), which only gave Israel political cover for sitting on its hands. Incrementalism runs against Palestinian interests as well because what they have to offer, peace, is not splittable into tradable chunks.

Besides ruling out a phased process, a highly asymmetric deal of the land-for-peace type requires either trust between the parties (nonexistent) or a mutually trusted arbiter with coercive power. Israel trusts only the US and coercion is not an option. . . .

The High Cost for Israel

Intangibility, irreversibility, asynchronicity, plus the lack of mutual trust or of a trusted enforcer: these are the strategic reasons all incremental approaches to the two-state solution have failed so far. . . . As if this were not enough, two more disincentives have kept Israel from playing along. One of them is the paradox that, by curbing terrorism, the separation barrier has diminished the short-term added value of peace, a commodity whose market price tends to vary in proportion to its distance to the buyer's present sense of security. . . . The other disincentive is Israel's lack of bargaining power. How so? To be effective, a peace agreement would require overwhelming support among Palestinians (whereas majority support in Israel would be sufficient). This . . . detail all but decimates Israel's bargaining power, as it presents it with a "binary" ne-

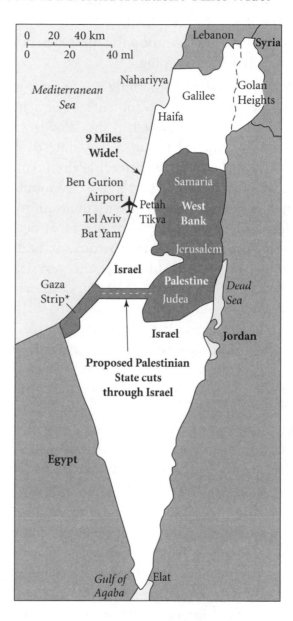

How Would You Defend A Nation 9 Miles Wide?

TAKEN FROM: Unity Coalition for Israel (UCI), http://
www.israelunitycoalition.org/maps/map_israel.jpg.

gotiating stand, where wresting the slightest concession quickly becomes counterproductive. Think of it as negotiating the purchase of a parachute: settling for half a parachute at half the price might be an option for the seller but not the buyer. For Israel, it's all or nothing.

What's wrong with "nothing"? Nothing, of course, is the current policy. It is also Zionism's[1] death march. So you'd think Israel would have ditched the "Road Map to Nowhere" long ago and hurried to cut a two-state deal. Ah, if only it could, but you've heard it before: [Palestinian Islamic fundamentalist organization] Hamas must recognize Israel; [Palestinian National Authority president Mahmoud] Abbas is a weakling; the terrorist infrastructure must be dismantled; etc. Hogwash. Israel drags its feet because it finds the peace pill unbearably bitter. How bitter? At the very least: dismantling 120 settlements; relocating 110,000 settlers; swapping pre-[19]67 land for settlement blocs already in Israeli hands; rerouting the separation barrier; ceding control over 40% of the West Bank; sharing Jerusalem as a capital; letting in 10–50 [thousand] refugees; giving away vital water rights; returning the Golan [Heights] to Syria (no comprehensive peace without it); engaging Hamas; facing violent domestic opposition; endangering the careers and lives of Israeli leaders; last but not least, implicitly admitting that two-thirds of Israel's history has been a monumental blunder. . . .

That said, critics of Israel tend to underestimate the barriers to peace. This is not an excuse but a statement of fact: the two-state solution demands of Israel the kind of concessions history wrests from nations defeated at war. Having been defeated at peace, not at war, Israel is psychologically unequipped for the task. All the giving must be, de facto [in reality], Israeli and the taking Palestinian—the neat thing about having noth-

---

1. Zionism is the political movement founded as an official organization in 1897 by Jewish journalist Theodor Herzl for the return of the Jewish people to their homeland and the establishment of a Jewish state in Palestine.

ing is that you have nothing to give. Of course, Israel would be "giving" nothing—only returning what it grabbed in contravention of international law—but it is indicative of its delusions of innocence that it should always speak of generous offers, never of legal redress. Peace requires quick, painful surgery. . . .

Dwindling Support

If Israel's 60th anniversary proves anything, it is that the Palestinian problem won't go away on its own. Sounding like a pyromaniac warning of the dangers of fire, [Israeli prime minister Ehud] Olmert put it bluntly: "If the day comes when the two-state solution collapses [. . .] the State of Israel is finished." Squelched in 1948, the two-state idea began to gain mutual acceptance barely two decades ago; it took 15 years for [Palestinian leader Yasser] Arafat to sell it to the PLO [Palestine Liberation Organization]. It was not even part of [the 1993] Oslo [Accords] and it has never captured the Palestinian imagination. Today, it elicits among Israelis not a sigh of hope but a collective yawn. The two-state solution may be that rare idea that goes directly from "futuristic" to "obsolete" without stopping at the intermediate stage called "timely."

Geopolitics is changing, too. [Islamic political and paramilitary organization] Hezbollah, Syria, and Iran, the region's ascending power, now loom larger in the Israeli psyche than the Palestinian conflict. Israel has never lost a war against the Palestinians but it got bloodied twice in Lebanon. Peace with Syria has a low cost/benefit ratio for Israel and it appears to be back on the agenda. A deal would frustrate Washington [the United States] because it wouldn't break the Tehran [Iran]-Damascus [Syria] axis, just as Jordan's normalization with Israel didn't hurt a bit its relations with [Iraqi leader] Saddam [Hussein] or Hamas. . . . America's waning influence in the region may prove a blessing. It may force Israel to ditch its endless excuses and realize it is powerful enough to take the risks of peace: deal with Syria; engage with Hamas; and, crucially, end the occupation. One can dream. The evidence is somewhat less oneiric [dreamlike]: unless Palestine accepts to become a client state of the US, Israel will never be leaned upon to set it free; and it won't do it of its own volition.

Approaching the two-state solution as an incremental exchange of piecemeal concessions is doomed. Outside coercion is ruled out, so a successful implementation would require of Israel to assume *voluntarily* the submissive posture of a vanquished nation: an unlikely scenario for a country unaccustomed to defeat and the behavioral exigencies that go with it. . . . The two-state solution calls for visionary leadership that Israel does not have, international prodding that is nonexistent, and an obliging enemy that has never much been the obliging kind. The final nail in the coffin might be its dwindling popular support.

> *"Jerusalem ... will never again be divided or cut in half. Jerusalem will remain only under Israel's sovereignty."*

Jerusalem Must Remain United Under Israeli Sovereignty

Benjamin Netanyahu

In the following viewpoint, Benjamin Netanyahu argues that to ensure future peace and guarantee that all religions have access to sacred sites, Jerusalem must be undivided and under Israeli sovereignty. Before Israel liberated Jerusalem in 1967, Netanyahu points out, its residents could not move freely from one place to another. Since then, he maintains the city has thrived and has become prosperous and alive, a holy city that attracts people from all over the world.

Benjamin Netanyahu is serving his second term as prime minister of Israel.

As you read, consider the following questions:

1. According to Netanyahu, what is the only way to guarantee that everyone continues to live in Jerusalem safely?

2. According to the author, what meaning did the liberation of Jerusalem and the Western Wall have for Jews?

3. According to Netanyahu, what prophecy has gradually been coming true since the unification of Jerusalem under Israel's flag and in what ways can this be seen in Jerusalem itself?

Last night I returned to Jerusalem, our capital, from a very important visit to Washington, capital of the United States. It was very important for me to come back to participate in this ceremony and say the same things I said in the United States:

United Jerusalem is the capital of Israel. Jerusalem has always been—and always will be—ours. It will never again be divided or cut in half. Jerusalem will remain only under Israel's sovereignty. In united Jerusalem, the freedom of worship and freedom of access for all three religions to the holy sites will be guaranteed, and it is the only way to guarantee that members of all faiths, minorities and denominations can continue living here safely. . . .

The Liberation of Jerusalem

For nineteen years Jerusalem was a wounded city; a city at the heart of which were barbed wires and minefields, firing posts and "no-man's lands"; a city whose main streets were covered with defensive walls against snipers; a city whose residents could not move freely from place to place. In June 1967, this situation changed forever. It changed in this place, on Ammunition Hill, and in other heroic battles inside Jerusalem.

You, fighters for the liberation of Jerusalem, with your bodies and with the blood of your comrades, pried open the chokehold, united the city together, and allowed Jerusalem to be reopened once again as a lively, vibrant city.

I enlisted shortly after the liberation of Jerusalem and I met with one of the fighters, who is here with us today, Nir

An International Norm

Keeping Jerusalem united and free under the sovereignty of Israel is not a break from international norms or practice. Historically, there have been international claims that other holy cities be internationalized as well. This was the case with Istanbul, the seat of Eastern Orthodox Christianity after the fall of the Ottoman Empire. Furthermore, some called for Mecca's internationalization after the Saudis captured the city in the 1920s, when Indian Muslims became concerned by the implications of Wahhabi rules for the practice of other Islamic traditions. But these challenges eventually abated. Ultimately, there is no reason why Israel's role in Jerusalem cannot come to be accepted as well.

Dore Gold, The Fight for Jerusalem, *2007.*

Nitzan. He did not voluntarily tell us; we had to repeatedly ask him to tell us what happened here, in that battle. Ultimately, quietly, shortly, dryly even, he told us a little of what took place here on that day, and we, as youngsters, stood in awe of the greatness of spirit, solidarity and sacrifice of those fighters who fought here, and the many others who fought in other places. The fighters who fell instilled pride in our people and gave us back our capital. As a boy, that day was etched in my memory. I remember the elation following the words of [the former chief of staff of the Israel Defense Forces] Motta Gur, when we heard the news on the radio and Motta Gur announced: "Har Habayit [site on which the Holy Temple stood] is in our hands!" The excitement we felt was something neither we nor any other Jew experienced for generations. It lifted the hearts of Jews all over the world.

A Jewish Dream Come True

Another remarkable thing happened: thousands, thousands of Israeli citizens, not only from Jerusalem, but from all over the country, rushed in masses into the Old City, passing through roads that were previously blocked, places we were never allowed to set foot in, through barbed wires, along the now shattered separation walls, climbing rocks and entering into back alleys—all of us heading towards the same place: the Western Wall. I remember that the square was narrow—in fact, there was no square at all—and the place was too narrow to contain the large masses, and each of us waited our turn to arrive at that ancient wall. I remember the beating of my heart and the exhilaration I felt when I first touched the stones of the Western Wall, thinking about King David, King Solomon, Israel's prophets and kings and the Maccabim [Maccabees]. I thought about the people of Israel throughout the generations, as did the thousands of Israelis who arrived there. The liberation of Jerusalem and the Western Wall marked for all of us the deep connection to the roots of Jewish history. We felt that the dream of generations had finally come true.

Thousands of years ago, a Psalms poet wrote: "built-up Jerusalem is like a city that is united together". It is as if this song was written now about the events of our generation.

Jerusalem Has Blossomed

Look around you and see how Jerusalem is built, how it is connected, how it grows and develops to the east and west, north and south. Jews, Muslims and Christians, religious and secular, ultra-orthodox and conservatives live here in peace and good neighborly relations.

Look around you and see how vibrant and full of life Jerusalem is, during the day and night. The houses of prayer and synagogues are filled, as are the cafes and recreational places.

But Jerusalem is not only a city of the day-to-day or night life. It is first and foremost a city of sanctity, a city of vision, a city of prayer; the eyes of the entire world are fixed on Jerusalem. As Isaiah prophesied: "it will happen in the end of days: The mountain of the Temple of the Almighty will be firmly established as the head of the mountains, and it will be exalted above the hills, and all the nations will stream to it . . . for from Zion will the Torah come forth, and the word of the Almighty from Jerusalem".

Since the unification of Jerusalem under Israel's flag, this prophecy has been gradually coming true. Never, in the thousands of years of its history, has Jerusalem been so great and remarkable, never did it have such freedom of worship for members of all faiths and such free access to all places of worship. Pilgrims, believers and visitors from all ends of the universe visit Jerusalem every day.

Fulfillment of a Prophecy

Our connection to Jerusalem is thousands of years old. As a people, we have never relinquished "the apple of our eye", the object of our prayers, our nation's capital, Jerusalem. Today, as a state, we are fulfilling this age-old yearning, this ancient wish.

The greatest hardships, exiles and difficulties in history could never dissuade us from pursuing the realization of the Jewish people's dream of generations—the establishment of a state in the land of Israel, with Jerusalem as its capital. This was the wish of every Jew in exile, at every community and in every prayer: "next year in built-up Jerusalem". I believe that only the reuniting of Jerusalem under Israeli sovereignty would enable us to quickly fulfill the second part of Isaiah's prophecy: "they shall beat their swords into plowshares . . . nation will not lift sword against nation and they will no longer learn how to wage warfare".

This is our prayer, and this is our hope here in Jerusalem.

> "Recognizing that Jerusalem is two cities
> is the first step to making peace with
> the Palestinians and the Arabs."

Control over Jerusalem Must Be Shared

Gershon Baskin

In the following viewpoint, Gershon Baskin argues that Jerusalem is not the united eternal capital of Israel. It is, he maintains, and has been since 1949, a divided city, one part Palestinian and the other Israeli. Israelis do not really care about the Palestinian parts of the city and must formally recognize that Jerusalem is not one but two cities, according to Baskin. He asserts that Jerusalem as two capitals is a workable solution and the first step toward peace.

Gershon Baskin is cochief executive officer of the joint Israeli-Palestinian think tank Israel/Palestine Center for Research and Information and a member of the leadership of Israel's Green Movement party.

As you read, consider the following questions:

1. According to Baskin, in what ways has Palestine been divided from 1949 to the present?

2. In the author's view, why is Palestine's being so segregated fortunate?

3. According to Baskin, why is de facto Muslim sovereignty over the Temple Mount entirely possible?

Not one country in the world recognizes our capital, Jerusalem, as the capital of Israel. Even the United States footnotes the following on the State Department Web page: Israel proclaimed Jerusalem as its capital in 1950. The US, like nearly all other countries, maintains its embassy in Tel Aviv. UN Security Council Resolution 478 declared the 1980 Jerusalem Law that declared Jerusalem to be Israel's "eternal and indivisible" capital null and void, affirming that it was a violation of international law.

The Reality: Two Jerusalems

The European Union is debating its own position on Jerusalem. The debate is a much better reflection of the reality of Jerusalem than any of the governing politicians in Jerusalem have the courage to admit. After lying to the public for 42 years about Jerusalem being the united eternal capital of Israel, it is time to admit there are two Jerusalems—one Israeli and one Palestinian. Even [former Jerusalem mayor] Teddy Kollek ..., admitted in 1988 that "coexistence in Jerusalem is dead." This was a great blow for the man who believed he had united the city.

Since the birth of the State of Israel, Jerusalem has never been united. From 1949 to 1967, it was divided by a wall and barbed wire, and since 1967 it has been divided politically, culturally, ethnically and nationally. While it is true that the massive Israeli annexation of land and building in what was once called east Jerusalem has changed the definitions of the division, with a near Jewish majority in east Jerusalem, the geography is not the proper definitive term. It is more correct to speak about Israeli Jerusalem and Palestinian Jerusalem.

The Two Options for Jerusalem

There are only two options for Jerusalem that I can live with. The first is if we go back to the 1967 borders and divide Jerusalem so that the eastern part—legally part of the occupied territories—becomes the capital of the Palestinian territories and the western part, which legally belongs to Israel, becomes the capital of Israel. The second option would be to keep the city unified and allow free access to Palestinians and Israelis and allow each side to have this unified city as its capital.

Ghassan Khatib, Moment, *March–April 2008.*

Israeli Attitude About Palestinian Jerusalem

Let's admit it to ourselves, we, as Israelis, don't really care about the Palestinian parts of Jerusalem. Even though they have been under our rule for the past 42 years, we don't treat them as equal parts of the city. They do not receive nearly the same services as Israeli neighborhoods. Their educational system is backward, underfunded, crowded and incapable of filling the needs of the people there. Today, one of Jerusalem's Palestinian neighborhoods, Kafr Akab, is located beyond the separation wall after the Kalandiya checkpoint.

We have to sincerely ask ourselves: Do we really want the Shuafat refugee camp as part of the eternal undivided capital of the State of Israel? To the best of my knowledge we do not chant: If I forget thee Umm Tuba [Arab neighborhood of east Jerusalem], let my right hand wither, or by the waters of Babylon, we sat and wept when we remembered thee, Jebl Mukaber [a mostly Arab neighborhood of east Jerusalem].

We do not say: Next year in [the Palestinian town of] Walaja and we certainly do not pray for the peace of [the

Arab village of] Sur Bahir. For [the Palestinian village of] Beit Hanina's sake, I will not be silent.

A Strategy for Jerusalem's Future

In a way, we are fortunate that the city is so segregated—it makes its political partition possible. As a member of prime minister Ehud Barak's expert committee on Jerusalem prior to the Taba [peace] summit in January 2001, we sat around a large aerial photograph and drew lines of division of sovereignty, based on the [2001 U.S. president Bill] Clinton parameters for Jerusalem which stated: what's Jewish to Israel, what's Arab to the Palestinians. We were instructed by the prime minister to design Israel's strategy for the future of Jerusalem on that basis, and it can be done.

Of course, the most sensitive part of Jerusalem is the Old City. It is less than one square kilometer [0.4 square miles] and is composed of four quarters—the Muslim (the largest quarter by far), Christian, Armenian and Jewish. There are two possible solutions for the Old City: a special international regime which would protect and guarantee the rights and the security of all within its walls or the application of the Clinton parameters to it as well—meaning that the Palestinians would have sovereignty over the Muslim, Christian and probably the Armenian quarters and Israel would have sovereignty over the Jewish Quarter.

The Temple Mount

The heart of the heart of Jerusalem is the Temple Mount/ Haram al-Sharif. For the Muslims, it is their third most holy place. Here Ibrahim [Abraham] brought Ishmael for sacrifice (according to their tradition) and here the prophet Muhammad ascended to heaven to begin receiving the revelation of the Koran [sacred writings of Islam]. For Muslims, the commandment of hajj [pilgrimage] is not complete until visiting Jerusalem after Mecca and Medina.

For Jews, it is the *most* holy place. Wherever Jews are in the world they face Jerusalem in prayer and within Jerusalem, they turn their prayers to the Temple Mount. Current and long-standing Halacha [collective body of Jewish law, custom, and tradition], and the decisions of the Chief Rabbinate and the important haredi [Orthodox] rabbis, is that Jews should not enter the Temple Mount. The reason is that we don't know the location of the Holy of Holies and the rabbis want to prevent the site from becoming impure.

Since 1967, Israel has claimed sovereignty over the Temple Mount, but in practice it is controlled by the Muslim authorities. It would be completely possible to turn the status quo into de facto Muslim sovereignty and from the Jewish point of view, we could easily say that when the messiah comes, the terms of sovereignty can be changed (if so desired by God).

Jerusalem Is the Key to Peace

Recognizing that Jerusalem is two cities is the first step to making peace with the Palestinians and the Arabs. Jerusalem should not be left for the end of the process. The Europeans got it right—peace begins with Jerusalem. The walls and fences that have been built in the city over the past years must come down. The only walls that should remain are those around the Old City.

Jerusalem will become a place of great international importance—when there are over 150 embassies in the city (that could serve two states) and it is open, modernized, environmentally conscious, as cities of international importance are. Then, it will not only be the city of peace [the literal meaning of its name], it will also be a much more pleasant city to live in.

Resolving that Jerusalem will be the capital of two states is not only doable, it is the only way that Jerusalem will be recognized as the capital of Israel.

Periodical Bibliography

*The following articles have been selected to supplement the
diverse views presented in this chapter.*

Ibrahim Alloush   "What Is Jerusalem?" *Star* (Amman, Jordan),
                         December 7, 2009.

Jerold S. Auerbach   "Which Two-State Solution? (Another View)
                         (Israel-Palestine dispute)," *Jewish Advocate*, June
                         12, 2009.

Daniel Doron   "Say No to a Palestinian State," *Forbes*, May 16,
                         2009.

Michael Dumper   "'Two State Plus': Jerusalem and the Bination-
                         alism Debate," *Jerusalem Quarterly*, Autumn
                         2009.

Dan Ephron   "Who Needs Peace, Love, and Understanding,
                         Anyway?" *Newsweek*, January 2, 2010.

Tom Gross   "Building Peace Without Obama's Interfer-
                         ence," *Wall Street Journal*, December 2, 2009.

William Nitze and   "EU Could Bring Peace to Middle East,"
Leon Hadar   *Guardian* (Manchester), December 4, 2009.

Shimon Peres   "One Region, Two States," *Washington Post*,
                         February 10, 2009.

Darya Shaikh   "Israelis and Palestinians Want Peace," *Guard-
                         ian* (Manchester), April 22, 2009.

OPPOSING
VIEWPOINTS®
SERIES

CHAPTER 4

What Should U.S. Policy Be Toward Israel?

Chapter Preface

In a private conversation in 1962, U.S. president John F. Kennedy spoke to Israeli foreign minister Golda Meir about U.S. relations with the then fifteen-year-old state of Israel. "The United States," he said, "has a special relationship with Israel in the Middle East, really comparable only to that which it has with Britain over a wide range of world affairs." Fifteen years later, another U.S. president—Jimmy Carter—used the term "special relationship" publicly for the first time when, during a press conference, he stated, "We have a special relationship with Israel. It's absolutely crucial that no one in our country or around the world ever doubt that our number one commitment in the Middle East is to protect the right of Israel to exist, to exist permanently, and to exist in peace."

The "special relationship" did not always exist and has been stronger and more accepted at some times than at others. In 1947, when the United Nations was considering the partition of Palestine, even though the United States pushed for partition, American diplomats stationed in the Middle East, as well as other government officials, cautioned against it. The next year, when President Harry S. Truman recognized the state of Israel eleven minutes after it was proclaimed, he did so strictly against the advice of the secretary of state, undersecretary of state, and other members of the State Department. Four years later, President Truman defended his decision, saying, "I had faith in Israel before it was established, I have faith in it now. I believe it has a glorious future before it—not just as another sovereign nation, but as an embodiment of the great ideals of our civilization."

U.S.-Israel relations during the early and mid-1950s, however, were restrained largely because of the interests of oil companies and the concerns of members of the State Department who favored Arab interests and positions in international affairs. The gradual move toward a closer U.S.-Israel strategic relationship began in the late 1950s, when the administration of President Dwight Eisenhower began to look at Israel as a strategic asset to the United States. The relationship deepened after the Six Day War of 1967 and the Yom Kippur War of 1973 and grew even stronger and became further entrenched following the 1979 peace accord with Egypt.

Historical, ethical, moral, and religious factors, as well as political and institutional ones, all have contributed to the special American-Israeli relationship. So have security, economic, and academic connections, and personal bonds between the two countries. Ties between the two countries are extensive and deep. This is not to say that over the years there has not been discord between the United States and Israel. As recently as 2010, the United States and Israeli governments became deeply divided over continued building of Israeli settlements in the West Bank and construction of Jewish housing in disputed areas of Jerusalem. At the time, according to Israeli ambassador to the United States Michael Oren, relations between the two countries had reached a historic crisis.

The United States' relationship with Israel has been a matter of debate since the Jewish nation first came into existence. In recent years, however, greater numbers of people have begun to speak out. Some believe that both the United States and Israel benefit from the special relationship and it must remain intact. Others believe that certain aspects of the relationship should change. Still others disagree entirely; they believe for a variety of reasons that the United States should end its special relationship with Israel. The viewpoints in this chapter reflect the differing views regarding the U.S.-Israel relationship.

"If [U.S.] aid were reduced to a point that Israel couldn't buy the equipment it needs to defend itself and maintain the peace, that would be dangerous to [the United States]."

The United States Should Give Aid to Israel

Middle East Quarterly

In the following viewpoint, four analysts discuss U.S. aid to Israel. The analysts argue over whether U.S. aid to Israel has become symbolic of their relationship and whether Israel could afford a cutoff of U.S. aid. One analyst concludes that if we were to reduce aid to Israel, it would ultimately be dangerous for the United States.

The Middle East Quarterly is a quarterly journal published by the Middle East Forum, an American conservative think tank.

As you read, consider the following questions:

1. By how much was U.S. aid to Israel reduced in 2000, according to the article?

Middle East Quarterly, "Debate: Continue U.S. Aid to Israel?" June 2000. Copyright © 2000 The Middle East Forum. Reproduced by permission.

2. According to the article, should the United States consider how the reduction of aid to Israel would appear to other nations?

3. Do the analysts in this viewpoint agree that there is no difference between the economic and security aid the United States gives to Israel?

A merican financial aid to Israel began in 1949 with a $100,000 trade loan and peaked in the mid-1990s at over $5 billion a year in grants and loans. Over fifty years, the total in grants and loans has amounted to $79 billion. Is the continuation of aid to Israel a good idea? If so, for how long should it go on? What criteria should it meet? Does an aid package of some $17 billion to help smooth the way for a peace treaty with Syria make sense? To assess these matters, the *Middle East Quarterly* invited four analysts [to discuss it]: Patrick Clawson is senior editor of the *Quarterly*; Ester Kurz is legislative strategy director of the American Israel Public Affairs Committee (AIPAC); Gwendolyn Mikell is a senior fellow for Africa at the Council on Foreign Relations; and Hillel Fradkin is resident scholar at the American Enterprise Institute. Robert Satloff, executive director of the Washington Institute for Near East Policy, moderated the discussion. They met in Washington on March 17, 2000.

Aid as a Symbol

Middle East Quarterly [MEQ]: Has aid become so symbolic of the U.S.-Israel relationship that Israel cannot afford its cutoff?

Patrick Clawson: Yes, and it's unfortunate that support for aid to Israel has become the most important indicator of whether or not one favors a close U.S.-Israel relationship. It would be good to disassociate the two, so that those who support a close relationship could take different positions on aid. We should find a currency other than cash by which to measure the strength of that relationship.

Ester Kurz: I disagree with the question's premise. Aid is less a symbol of the U.S.-Israel relationship than it is a real benefit to the United States and Israel. We give aid to Israel to maintain its security in a very tough region and a very important part of the world in order to advance critical U.S. interests. If that aid were reduced to a point that Israel couldn't buy the equipment it needs to defend itself and maintain the peace, that would be dangerous to us.

Furthermore, the U.S. and Israel have agreed on a plan where aid is in fact going down each year. It was reduced by $60 million two years ago [in 1998], by $120 million last year, and by $180 million this year. So it's already being looked at in terms of its concrete value to Israel and to the United States.

Gwendolyn Mikell: I have heard from constituencies that are aware that there is a lot of symbolism in aid to Israel. They understand the importance of maintaining Israel's security, but many of them are saying: "Couldn't we do that in ways that don't always involve cash?" Notice: I didn't say do away with aid to Israel. But many people are arguing that, in the current environment, some of the aid to Israel could be used more productively in non-Western regions like Africa, where needs are great and, believe it or not, American security interests are also important. While they support Israel, they'd love to see a sharing of the resources that are being used there.

Kurz: I would argue for increasing rather than redistributing the same-sized pie. We're the greatest country in the world, and we should be able to meet our international obligations wherever they may be. We have the resources. When you look at what we're spending on defense versus what we're spending on foreign aid, it's very unfortunate.

Hillel Fradkin: To return to the initial question: Do we need some way other than aid to express the relationship between United States and Israel? It would be nice, but as a symbolic matter, financial aid has come to be identified with the closeness of that relationship; so, we have to ask how it would appear to other countries if it were substantially reduced. The reductions that have taken place are fairly small. The alternatives to aid might involve security arrangements that could restrict the independence of both the United States and Israel. That makes it hard to find a substitute means of symbolizing the relationship. . . .

Aid Comes Back to the United States

MEQ: Is there really a difference between the economic and security aid we give to Israel?

Kurz: No, because it's all security-related. The economic aid repays prior American military loans to Israel. So it's all security aid, no matter what it's called.

Clawson: I agree: The distinction between the two is not useful or meaningful. The economic aid that we give Israel is a simple cash grant. It's not as though we finance specific projects that otherwise wouldn't happen. Israel gets a certain amount of cash from the United States each year and that's how we ought to think of it.

Kurz: And the money goes right back to the United States to pay the loans that Israel took out for military purchases.

| *"Every cent we give Israel is in violation of the Foreign Assistance Act."*

The United States Should End Aid to Israel

Stephanie Westbrook

In the following viewpoint, Stephanie Westbrook explains that she is surprised and dismayed by the amount of U.S. taxpayer money the United States gives Israel annually. She argues that no one in Congress seems to have the courage to touch the military aid package, which is being used illegally for weapons and arms and could be put to better use at home. Westbrook maintains that more Americans need to question not only foreign aid to Israel but the special U.S.-Israel relationship in general.

Stephanie Westbrook is a U.S. citizen living in Rome, Italy, where she is active in peace and social justice movements.

As you read, consider the following questions:

1. What percentage of Israel's annual defense budget is funding from the United States, according to Westbrook?

2. According to the author, what two acts is the United States violating by giving Israel military aid and selling it arms?

3. According to *New York Times* columnist Roger Cohen,
cited by Westbrook, what also makes the U.S.-Israel relationship special?

A "regional economic power." That's how ANIMA, the
Euro-Mediterranean Network of Investment Promotion
Agencies encompassing 70 governmental agencies and international networks, described Israel in its January 2010 *Mediterranean Investment Map*. The report analyzed the economies of
the 27 European Union countries as well as 9 "partner countries."

And who can argue? Touting an annual GDP [gross domestic product] growth rate around 5% for the years 2004 to
2008, Israel was also ranked 27 out of 132 countries in the
World Economic Forum's *Global Competitiveness Report* last
fall [in 2009]. It ranked 9th for innovative capacity.

In the 2008 *World Competitiveness Yearbook* by IMD [a
business school in Switzerland], Israel comes in 2nd for the
number of scientists and engineers in the workforce. No other
country in the world spends more on research and development as a percentage of GDP than Israel. Since the year 2000
it has hovered around 4.5%, or twice the average of OECD
[Organisation for Economic Co-operation and Development]
member countries.

U.S. Taxpayer Money Misspent

I am not an economist, but I have to wonder why US taxpayers are doling out $3 billion a year in direct military aid to a
"regional economic power." In August 2007, a Memorandum
of Understanding between the US and Israel was signed committing the US to give, not loan, $30 billion to Israel over 10
years. US taxpayers are directly funding close to 20% of Israel's
annual defense budget. No wonder Israel is able to invest in
R&D [research and development]!

To help put these figures into perspective, a new web site
was launched [in February 2010] that illustrates how your

state is contributing to the Israeli defense budget and what could have instead been done with the money. At www.aid toisrael.org I learned that my home state of Texas will give more than $2.5 billion over the ten year period. For the same amount, over 2 million people could have been provided with primary health care.

At the 2007 signing ceremony for the $30 billion giveaway, then Under Secretary of State for Political Affairs Nicholas Burns, stated, "We consider this 30 billion dollars in assistance to Israel to be an investment in peace." But peace isn't exactly what we've gotten for our money.

An Investment in Weapons, Not Peace

Instead our tax dollars continue to pay for advanced weaponry used to maintain an illegal occupation, culminating a year ago in the [2009] Israeli attack on Gaza with US-made F-16 fighter jets, US-made Apache helicopter gunships, US-made naval combat ships, US-made hellfire missiles, US-made tanks and armored personnel carriers, and US-made white phosphorus shells.

Every cent we give Israel is in violation of the Foreign Assistance Act, which specifically prohibits aid to countries that "engage in a consistent pattern of gross violations of internationally recognized human rights." Sales of US weaponry made to Israel are in violation of the Arms Export Control Act, which restrict their use to legitimate self-defense.

Special Conditions for Israel

But weapons we do continue to sell, and aid we do continue to give. And if that wasn't enough, we also provide Israel with special conditions. Unlike all other countries receiving military aid from the US, Israel receives its entire bundle in a lump sum during the first 30 days of the fiscal year. The money sits in an interest bearing account at the Federal Reserve, the in-

Recent U.S. Aid to Israel

(millions of dollars)

Year	Total	Military Grant	Economic Grant	Immig. Grant	ASHA*	All Other
1949–1996	68,030.90	29,014.9	23,122.4	868.9	121.40	14,903.3
1997	3,132.10	1,800.0	1,200.0	80.0	2.10	50.0
1998	3,080.00	1,800.0	1,200.0	80.0	—	—
1999	3,010.00	1,860.0	1,080.0	70.0	—	—
2000	4,131.85	3,120.0	949.1	60.0	2.75	—
2001	2,876.05	1,975.6	838.2	60.0	2.25	—
2002	2,850.65	2,040.0	720.0	60.0	2.65	28.0
2003	3,745.15	3,086.4	596.1	59.6	3.05	—
2004	2,687.25	2,147.3	477.2	49.7	3.15	9.9
2005	2,612.15	2,202.2	357.0	50.0	2.95	—
2006	2,534.50	2,257.0	237.0	40.0	—	0.5
2007	2,500.20	2,340.0	120.0	40.0	2.95	0.2
2008	2,423.90	2,380.0	0.0	40.0	3.90	0.0
2009	2,550.00	2,550.0	0.0	?	?	0.0
Total	**106,164.70**	**58,573.4**	**30,897.0**	**1,558.2**	**144.20**	**14,991.9**

*American Schools and Hospitals Abroad Program

TAKEN FROM: Jeremy M. Sharp, "U.S. Foreign Aid to Israel," December 4, 2009. http://www.fas.org/sgp/mideast/RL33222.pdf.

terest going to Israel, of course, until 74% of it is funneled back to US weapons manufacturers in the way of purchases for the Israeli Defense ministry. Israel is free to use the remaining 24% to purchase "in house" weapons systems, an arrangement afforded to no other recipient of US military aid.

While we may hear some calls to freeze (or limit or curb) settlement construction, and as of late, for an end to the siege of Gaza, one subject no one on Capitol Hill dares to touch is this massive military aid package given to Israel. The new self-proclaimed "pro-peace pro-Israel" lobby, J-street, has said the subject is not up for discussion.

A Debatable Relationship

But some are starting to question our "special relationship" with Israel. On February 9 [2010], Intelligence Squared, the British debate forum, held a debate in New York City, home to the country's largest Jewish community asking if the "US should step back from its special relationship with Israel." Prior to the start of the debate, audience members cast their votes electronically, with 39% in favor, 42% against and 25% undecided.

Arguing for the motion were British author and *New York Times* columnist Roger Cohen and Columbia [University] professor and author Rashid Khalidi. Former US ambassador to the EU [European Union] Stuart Eizenstat and former Israeli ambassador to the US Itamar Rabinovich argued against. Cohen spoke of US aid to Israel:

"What also makes the relationship special is the incredible largess that the United States shows towards Israel, over the past decade, $28.9 billion in economic aid. And on top of that, another $30 billion in military aid, that's almost $60 billion. That's 10 times the GNP [gross national product] of Haiti that is being gifted to a small country. Now, I ask you, to what end is this money being used? Ladies and gentlemen, we would submit that it ends often inimical to the American interest."

Following the debate, the audience once again voted on the resolution, this time with a slight majority in favor, 49% for, 47% against and 4% undecided.

The "special relationship" is hereby up for discussion. Pass the word.

| "*Every country in the Middle East, and perhaps even the world, sees the United States as being the key to achieving peace [in Israel]."*

The United States Must Help Resolve the Israeli-Palestinian Conflict

King Abdullah II of Jordan

In the following viewpoint, King Abdullah II of Jordan contends that the United States has a stated, strategic interest in resolving the Israeli-Arab conflict. He contends that the United States must take the lead and use all its influence to foster a timely peace in accordance with parameters set forth in the Arab Peace Initiative. According to Abdullah, U.S. leadership can advance peace by understanding the region-wide framework for action, reinforcing the foundation for peace, and ensuring that U.S. actions send the right message, especially in response to Palestinian suffering.

King Abdullah II has been monarch of the Hashemite Kingdom of Jordan since 1999.

King Abdullah II of Jordan, "Remarks by His Majesty King Abdullah II," Embassy of Jordan, Washington, DC, Information Bureau, April 24, 2009. Reproduced by permission.

As you read, consider the following questions:

1. What is the one vital function King Abdullah II says the United States can perform immediately and what two steps does it involve?
2. According to the author, what groundwork is in place for an Arab-Israeli peace settlement?
3. According to King Abdullah II, what must the United States do to move forward after its good beginning?

Today I want to talk about the Palestinian-Israeli conflict, which has almost defined the modern history of my region. But I do not want to talk about missed opportunities. I want to focus on the urgency of not missing any more . . . and on why, and how, the United States can lead.

The US has a stated, strategic interest in ending this conflict. Few crises in history have presented such a potent mix of threats—from the regional instability and violence it promotes—to the worldwide divisions it has caused, divisions actively exploited by extremists. But, there have been equally few situations where a just solution could bring such powerful benefits—not only to the parties, not only to the region, but to the world as a whole.

The US Commitment to Middle East Peace

Yet time . . . is not on our side. Every day we lose makes the conflict much harder to resolve. And that is a danger to all of us.

I know this is understood by President [Barack] Obama and his team. The President gave early signals that Middle East peace will be a priority for the United States. We in Jordan welcome his commitment and engagement. And we are not alone. Every country in the Middle East, and perhaps even the world, sees the United States as being the key to achieving peace. America's strategic interests will be advanced by a peace settlement . . . and in the eyes of the world, American credibility will be advanced as well.

Tackling the issue, head-on, is now imperative. Success urgently demands, not more process, but more results. That means a clear plan to reach a comprehensive peace—one that builds on the achievements of previous negotiations. And there must also be a vigorous leadership commitment, to ensure negotiations move fast, towards reconciliation on the basis of the two-state solution.

The Need for a Just Settlement

We do not have time to engage in yet another open-ended process. We have seen what comes of process without progress. Every missed opportunity has alienated more people on both sides. Such a course increases distrust and difficulties and fuels those who seek to carry the parties down the path of confrontation.

Yet this path cannot help either party get where it needs to be. For Palestinians to reap the promise of the 21st century, for Israelis to achieve the enduring security they seek, there must be an end . . . to occupation and confrontation . . . to settlement-building . . . to unilateral actions in Jerusalem. There must be a settlement that fulfils the legitimate rights of both parties—the right of Palestinians to statehood, and the right of Israelis to security.

The US Role

One of the vital functions the United States can play right now, is to help its friends think and act in these strategic terms. That means keeping the focus on where the parties want to be—in ten, twenty, thirty years and more; the hopes and horizons for themselves and their children—and then setting a direction towards that future, now.

Through its own focus, through its own resolve, the United States will set the standard. Events are already testing American credibility. These include the Israeli voices for turning back the clock on negotiations—to disestablish the established agenda for peace. And they include extremist voices in the Arab world that preach war. I hope that the United States will make it clear that it will not accept retrograde movement. The elements of a settlement are known; the agenda for negotiations is agreed; there is a clear objective: Two states, each sovereign, viable, and secure. Such a settlement is a vital US interest, and it is equally vital to [US] interests that the world see the US lead the way.

Parameters of the Arab Peace Initiative

Indeed, the groundwork is there. The two-state settlement has been agreed by the parties and the entire international community. And for seven years, against all provocation, the landmark Arab Peace Initiative has held. The initiative lays out the parameters of a comprehensive settlement—ending the occupation . . . creating a Palestinian state . . . and providing security guarantees and normal relations for Israel. Muslim countries around the world have also expressed their support. This offers Israel a place in its neighbourhood and more: acceptance by the one-third of the UN members—that's 57 countries—that still do not recognize Israel.

By its unanimous voice, by its serious approach, the Arab Peace Initiative is the most important proposal for peace in the history of this conflict. We have made our choice: a comprehensive peace that meets the legitimate needs of all. Israel now has to make its choice. To integrate into the region, accepted and accepting, with normal relations with its neighbours. Or to remain fortress Israel, isolated, and holding itself and the entire region a hostage to continuing confrontation.

And let me be clear: any Israeli effort to substitute Palestinian development for Palestinian independence cannot bring peace and stability to the region. The path for peace can go only through the two-state solution. No other solution can offer the justice that people demand and expect. And no other solution can give people a reason to take the risks peace requires.

An Urgent Need to Act

Israel must know that attempting to delay this solution will be disastrous for its own future as well as for the future of the Palestinians. I cannot emphasize enough how important US partnership is, to help Israel accept the opening the Arab world has offered, work with us, and move forward.

Now is the time for the United States to lead, to ensure that no more time is wasted. Failing to act means that we will all lose. The status quo is simply untenable. The dangers are too many and too big to ignore. A moment of truth is here, for all who claim to seek peace and justice. It is a time for partnership, courage and action.

The Goal: Peace, Not a Process

It begins with an effective peace plan . . . —a plan of negotiations that can achieve concrete results quickly, and stop a drift towards confrontation. I say plan, not process, for a reason. The very term "peace process" is an [artifact] of history. When it was coined in the 1970s, the idea was to break the decades of deadlock by taking an incremental approach. And in the following decades we did see breakthroughs. Great leaders, like my late father His Majesty King Hussein and [Israeli] Prime Minister Yitzhak Rabin, gave their all to make progress happen.

Today, I do not diminish those achievements when I say that this old idea has seen its day. The peace process must end, because we have reached the time for the end-game, in which all sides can win.

Allow me to touch on some areas where creative US leadership can advance that goal.

United States Indispensable for Arab-Israeli Peace

When I speak publicly about Arab-Israeli diplomacy, I always ask my audience why, despite our current diminished credibility, America's phone is still ringing with pleas from the Arabs, the UN, and the Europeans to be more involved in Arab-Israeli diplomacy. Nobody in the audience ever seems to know or at least volunteer the answer, but it's so obvious to me. The fact is that we are indispensable to a resolution of the issue precisely because of our close ties to Israel. Everyone and his mother has good relations with the Arabs. America is the only power that has both sides covered. . . . It is our capacity to gain Israel's confidence and trust, which allows us to cajole and pressure, that makes us a compelling and attractive mediator.

Aaron David Miller, The Much Too Promised Land, *2008.*

Three Key Areas for US Leadership

First is in understanding the region-wide framework for action. The Palestinian-Israeli conflict does not take place in a vacuum. Regional crises and events are deeply interconnected. Successful policy must be part of a holistic approach. This includes a division of labour with regional partners. One example is the work Arab states are already doing to encourage Palestinian reconciliation. International support will advance this effort. In this and similar actions, US policy can help empower the region's forces of moderation.

A second key area for US leadership is reinforcing the foundation for peace. Development aid will not succeed if it is designed as a substitute for Palestinian independence. But independence will be most successful when it delivers opportunities for fruitful, normal daily life. Benefits and incentives need to be devised that will create and sustain the conditions for co-existence and progress.

A third area for US leadership is in the powerful messages [its] actions can send—especially, by your response to Palestinian suffering. Signals are delivered when the US ensures relief and rebuilding in Gaza, and provides humanitarian aid in the West Bank. But signals are also sent when [the United States] acts, or fails to act, against the daily hardships of West Bank life . . . against illegal settlement building . . . against Israeli actions to force Jerusalem's Arab, Muslim and Christian population out or threaten Muslim and Christian holy sites. The US commitment to Palestinian statehood must be unambiguous, in deeds as well as words. This is central to America's standing, not only in the region, but the entire Muslim world.

Continued US Effort and Support Needed

Let me say, Arabs and Muslims throughout the world took note of the President's inaugural pledge, for a new partnership based on mutual respect and mutual interest. His out-reach since then has been well received in the Arab world.

This good beginning needs to move forward without any break. A high-level US effort is needed to regenerate bilateral negotiations. And when the parties get to the table, US support must continue. Where there is deadlock, let the US break the impasse by proposing its own creative solutions. Beginning to end, the focus must be a final peace agreement; one that reflects the only viable solution to this conflict . . . the two-state solution, which will open the door to comprehensive Middle East peace.

A Jordan and US Partnership

This year [2009] marks 60 years of diplomatic ties between Jordan and the United States. Our partnership has been tested by crises. We have talked truth to each other . . . listened to each other . . . and worked together. We have had differences. This is the way of friends. But we have never lost sight of the value of our strategic partnership, or the vital goals we share: peace, prosperity, security.

Today, we stand together at yet another critical moment. The regional problems are complex and real. But in our world, we have seen rapid, positive transformations when strategic interests are clear. The parties, the region, the world, all deeply need this peace. And all are watching to see how America will lead.

I believe that peace can succeed—and we should settle for nothing less. In that effort, I pledge Jordan's continued partnership. And just as we ask the parties to do, let the friends of peace, too, think ahead, to the strategic picture. Ten years from now, meeting here, we could be, we should be, talking about the challenges of life after peace . . . and how to advance our new era of global co-existence. But to do that in the year 2019, we must also be able to say: our countries did what needed to be done, back in 2009, with courage and action.

> "U.S. policy toward Palestine is costly, a
> waste of time, and of no help to the
> real interests of the Palestinian or
> Israeli people."

The United States Should Not Help Resolve the Israeli-Palestinian Conflict

Ivan Eland

In the following viewpoint, Ivan Eland contends that the United States is not helping the Israelis or the Palestinians by being involved in the Arab-Israeli conflict. He argues that America is not impartial as it favors Israel and allows the Israeli government to maintain the upper hand in their relationship. According to Eland, the United States should spend its time dealing with other, more important issues instead of worrying about a conflict that is not going to be solved anytime soon.

Ivan Eland is an author and senior fellow and director of the Center on Peace & Liberty at the Independent Institute, a non-profit think tank.

Ivan Eland, "The Israeli-Palestinian Conflict—Why the U.S. Should Care Less," *Independent Institute*, June 1, 2009. Copyright © 2009 by the Independent Institute. Reproduced by permission of The Independent Institute, 100 Swan Way, Oakland, CA 94621-1428 USA. www.independent.org.

As you read, consider the following questions:

1. According to Eland, why will the Israelis not accommodate the U.S. request to halt Israeli settlements in the West Bank?

2. Why, according to the author, is what Israel does more a domestic issue than a national security concern for the United States?

3. According to Eland, what effect has the huge amounts of U.S. aid and political support had on the Israeli incentive to give Palestinians land?

[U.S. secretary of state] Hillary Clinton's blunt public statement that President [Barack] Obama "wants to see a stop to settlements—not some settlements, not outposts, not natural growth exceptions" made for good headlines. The Israelis were shocked and upset that their slavish ally had acted slightly less obsequious and engaged in a public spat with them.

This ballyhooed baby step came after Obama had raised halting Israeli settlements in the West Bank privately with hawkish Israeli Prime Minister Benjamin Netanyahu at the White House—only to get the push back that, at minimum, Israel would have to allow the "natural growth" of settlements to match population expansion.

Not a Modest Request

Yet Obama is only one of a string of U.S. presidents, beginning with Ronald Reagan, to press the Israelis to stop such settlement activity. Despite billions in U.S. military and economic aid to Israel, the Israelis won't even accommodate this seemingly modest U.S. request.

That's because the request is not modest and cuts to the heart of Israeli strategy. With current demographic trends, even many on the Israeli right realize that Israel will eventually have to acquiesce to a two-state solution. If the West Bank and Gaza aren't jettisoned, Arab population expansion, which is higher than Jewish growth, will eventually make the Jews minority rulers in an ostensibly democratic state—similar to apartheid South Africa. Thus, if democracy with a Jewish majority is to be preserved, the Palestinians will have to be given some sort of a state.

The Effects of Delay

That said, the longer that outcome can be delayed, the better for Israel because proliferating and expanding Jewish settlements can continue—thereby grabbing greater amounts of the best Palestinian land and leaving the Palestinians the meager scraps. Any affirmative Israeli response to U.S. pressure to halt settlements would ruin this underlying Israeli strategy of getting more Palestinian land while the gettin's good.

Of course, these continued Israeli salami tactics have weakened the moderate Palestinian leadership, who has nothing to show for its years of negotiation with Israel, and vastly strengthened the more strident [radical Islamic fundamentalist organization] Hamas, which does not acknowledge Israel's right to exist. Thus, Israel may wait too long to accept and implement the two-state solution so that it is no longer possible. Thus, the Israelis will be forced to give up their ideal of a Jewish democracy for an apartheid-style minority rule.

Why Should the United States Care?

But the real question may be why the United States should care. For the U.S., what Israel does is more a domestic issue than a national security concern. After the Cold War, a U.S. alliance with Israel gets the United States very little and merely antagonizes Middle Eastern oil producing nations. Although the United States gives Israel billions in aid every year, Israel is in the driver's seat in the bilateral relationship because U.S.

politicians—both Democratic and Republican—feel they need the support of the powerful Israeli lobby to get elected.

The moral claim that Israel is a small, embattled democracy surrounded by Arab dictatorships is nullified by the fact that much of Israel sits on land stolen by force of arms. Prior to the ethnic cleansing of Arabs before and during Israel's 1948 "war for independence," Jews owned only seven percent of the land in Palestine. After the ethnic cleansing, Jews possessed more than 70 percent of that land. Thus, like much of the land that is now the United States, even Israel proper was stolen from indigenous peoples and will not be given back. Israel, contrary to the myth of the David among Goliaths, has always been much stronger militarily than the Arabs and will not return Israel proper. So the United States has focused on getting the Palestinians some scrap of land that Israel might someday be willing to give up.

The Insanity of U.S. Policy

But why? On the one hand, the many U.S. presidential administrations—including that of Barack Obama—have pressured Israel to give the Palestinians land, and on the other hand—with huge amounts of military and economic aid and unflinching political support—they have made it less likely that Israel will do so. Albert Einstein said that doing the same thing over and over again and expecting a different result is insanity. U.S. policy is therefore insane. The Israeli-Palestinian conflict is not going to be solved anytime soon and worrying about it deflects the Obama administration's attention from more important problems.

Likewise, Palestinians continue to hope and expect the United States to pressure Israel to give them a state. But given U.S. domestic politics, the U.S. government is incapable of being an honest broker and therefore is unlikely to be of real help to the Palestinians.

U.S. Policy: More Harm than Good

Finally, massive U.S. aid and knee-jerk political support for Israel merely helps the Israelis continue their dysfunctional policy. If they would give up occupied land and settle the Palestinian issue, they could have much better relations with all of their Arab neighbors. Everyone in the region could get richer together.

Thus, U.S. policy toward Palestine is costly, a waste of time, and of no help to the real interests of the Palestinian or Israeli people. The United States should follow the physician's motto of "do no harm" and withdraw from the field.

Periodical Bibliography

The following articles have been selected to supplement the diverse views presented in this chapter.

Roni Bart "Cut US Aid to Israel," Ynetnews, July 18, 2008. www.ynetnews.com.

Gershon Baskin "An American Peace Initiative: (Is there a Nice Way of Saying 'An Imposed Solution'?)," *Tikkun*, January–February 2010.

Alon Ben-Meir "Obama's Peace Offensive (Part I) (Part II)," *Huffington Post*, July 28, 2009. www.huffington post.com.

Robert Dreyfuss "Still the Chosen One?" *Mother Jones*, September–October 2009.

Norman Finkelstein "It's Not Either/Or: The Israel Lobby," *Counter-Punch*, May 1, 2006. www.counterpunch.org.

Rachelle Marshall "Obama Must Choose Between Peace and the 'Special Relationship,'" *Washington Report on Middle East Affairs*, January–February 2010.

Henry Siegman "Imposing Middle East Peace," *Nation*, January 25, 2010.

Jerome Slater "Does Obama Understand the Israeli-Palestinian Conflict?" *Huffington Post*, January 11, 2010. www.huffingtonpost.com.

James Traub "The New Israel Lobby," *New York Times Magazine*, September 13, 2009.

For Further Discussion

Chapter 1

1. Yehuda Avner and David Wearing both talk about two separate principles: Israel's right to exist and recognition of Israel's right to exist. Do you think someone can say that Israel has a right to exist yet refuse to recognize that right? Why or why not?

2. Avi Sagi and Yedidia Stern argue that preserving Israel's definition as a Jewish state is essential. Oren Ben-Dor argues that Israel should not exist as a Jewish state and that the Palestinians should not recognize its right to do so. What are the strengths and weaknesses of each argument? Whose argument is stronger? Why?

Chapter 2

1. Jonathan Sacks contends that based on history, attachment, and long association the Jewish people have a right to the land of Israel. Susan Abulhawa argues that historically, legally, culturally, ethnically, and genetically the Palestinians have a right to the same land. Whose argument do you find more convincing? Why?

2. Nimer Sultany argues that Israel is an apartheid state because its Palestinian Arab citizens are "granted an inferior citizenship and face a separate and unequal reality." Based on the information in the viewpoint, what do you think? After reading Robbie Sabel's viewpoint, did your opinion change? If so, why, and in what way? If not, why not?

3. Based on the diametrically opposed arguments put forth by Richard L. Cravatts and Salman Abbu Sitta regarding the Palestinian right to return, what type of compromise plan do you think might help resolve the issue? If you

believe there can be no compromise, explain your reasoning.

Chapter 3

1. Hubertus Hoffmann believes that peace for Palestinians and Israelis can be achieved if a new power base is established by the Palestinians and a new peace policy based on a double strategy of power and reconciliation is instituted. Do you believe Hoffmann's plan is realistic? Give your reasons.

2. According to Charles Krauthammer, Hamas is playing a waiting game and has no intention of permanently living in peace with the Israelis. According to Ziad Khalil Abu Zayyad, Israel uses security as a rationale and is unwilling to make the compromises necessary for peace. Given their supporting arguments, do you think peace is possible in the near future? Why or why not?

3. Tzipi Livni believes that a two-state solution will serve the interests of both Israelis and Palestinians and resolve their conflict. Bernard Chazelle contends that Israel will not accept a two-state solution. If you were Tzipi Livni, how would you respond to Chazelle's supporting arguments?

4. Benjamin Netanyahu argues that Jerusalem is a united city and the capital of Israel. Gershon Baskin argues that Jerusalem is two cities and is not recognized by other nations as the capital of Israel. Which argument is based on fact? On opinion? How do you know?

Chapter 4

1. King Abdullah II of Jordan argues that the United States must take the lead in bringing an end to the Israeli-Palestinian conflict and achieving peace in the Middle East. Based on his interpretation of what would constitute a just solution and peace, do you agree that the United States should take a leading role? Why or why not?

2. Ivan Eland argues that U.S. aid and support of Israel, as well as U.S. policy toward Palestine, does more harm than good and that the United States should not be involved in the Israeli-Palestinian conflict. How persuasive is Eland's argument? What information might Eland have included to make it more persuasive?

Organizations to Contact

The editors have compiled the following list of organizations concerned with the issues debated in this book. The descriptions are derived from materials provided by the organizations. All have publications or information available for interested readers. The list was compiled on the date of publication of the present volume; the information provided here may change. Be aware that many organizations take several weeks or longer to respond to inquiries, so allow as much time as possible.

American Israel Public Affairs Committee (AIPAC)
440 First St. NW, Suite 600, Washington, DC 20001
(202) 639-5200 • fax: (202) 638-0680
Web site: www.aipac.org

AIPAC is a national member organization that acts as a pro-Israel lobby by working with U.S. political leaders to enact public policy that strengthens the U.S.-Israel relationship. AIPAC publications include the biweekly *Near East Report*, which may be downloaded from the AIPAC Web site. The Web site also provides links to backgrounders, analysis, and special reports on key issues affecting the Middle East, Israel's security, and the U.S.-Israel relationship.

American-Israeli Cooperative Enterprise (AICE)
2810 Blaine Dr., Chevy Chase, MD 20815
(301) 565-3918 • fax: (301) 587-9056
e-mail: mgbard@aol.com
Web site: www.jewishvirtuallibrary.org

AICE seeks to strengthen the relationship between Israel and the United States by emphasizing common values, developing cooperative social and educational programs that address shared domestic problems, and publicizing innovative Israeli solutions to these problems. The AICE Web site includes the Jewish Virtual Library, a comprehensive online encyclopedia of Jewish history and culture.

American Jewish Committee (AJC)
165 E. Fifty-sixth St., New York, NY   10022-2746
(212) 751-4000 • fax: (212) 891-1450
e-mail: pr@ajc.org
Web site: www.ajc.org

AJC works to strengthen U.S.-Israel relations, build international support for Israel, and support the Israeli-Arab peace process. AJC's numerous publications, which take many forms and are available for downloading or viewing at its Web site, include such titles as "Historical, Legal, and Political Aspects of Israeli Settlement Policy," and "The New Realism: American Jews' Views About Israel."

Americans for Middle East Understanding (AMEU)
475 Riverside Dr., Room 245, New York, NY   10115-0245
(212) 870-2053 • fax: (212) 870-2050
e-mail: info@ameu.org
Web site: www.ameu.org

AMEU works to foster a better understanding in the United States of the history, goals, and values of Middle Eastern cultures and peoples, the rights of Palestinians, and the forces shaping U.S. policy in the Middle East. AMEU publishes the bimonthly newsletter the *Link* and provides for sale numerous books, pamphlets, and videos on Israel, the Palestinians, and the Israeli-Palestinian conflict.

Foundation for Middle East Peace (FMEP)
1761 N St. NW, Washington, DC   20036
(202) 835-3650 • fax: (202) 835-3651
e-mail: info@fmep.org
Web site: www.fmep.org

FMEP promotes, through various activities, a just solution to the Israeli-Palestinian conflict. It publishes the bimonthly "Report on Israeli Settlements in the Occupied Territories," as well as analysis and commentary from other sources. The FMEP Web site provides links to maps, reference materials, and other resources.

Institute for Palestine Studies (IPS)

3501 M St. NW, Washington, DC   20007
(202) 342-3990 • fax: (202) 342-3927
e-mail: ipsdc@palestine-studies.org
Web site: www.palestine-studies.org

IPS is an independent academic organization devoted exclusively to documentation, research, analysis, and publication on Palestinian affairs and the Arab-Israeli conflict. It provides accurate information and analysis on Palestinian affairs and the Arab-Israeli conflict through such publications as the *Journal of Palestine Studies*, and *Jerusalem Quarterly* as well as such documents as "Quarterly Updates on Conflict and Democracy."

Israel Democracy Institute (IDI)

4 Pinsker St., Jerusalem   91046
   Israel
972 2 530-0888 • fax: 972 2 530-0837
Web site: www.idi.org.il

IDI is an independent nonpartisan research institute that devises ways to strengthen the moral and structural foundations of Israeli democracy. Its publications include the monthly *Terrorism and Democracy Newsletter* and policy papers written by its fellows and research assistants.

Israel Ministry of Foreign Affairs

9 Yitzhak Rabin Blvd., Jerusalem   91035
972 2 530-3111 • fax: 972 2 530-3367
e-mail: pniot@mfa.gov.il
Web site: www.mfa.gov.il

The ministry is the Israeli government agency that implements Israel's foreign policy and promotes economic, cultural, and scientific relations with other countries. Its Web site features facts about Israel, information about its history, historical documents, and more.

Middle East Forum (MEF)
1500 Walnut St., Suite 1050, Philadelphia, PA   19102
(215) 546-5406 • fax: (215) 546-5409
e-mail: info@meforum.org
Web site: www.meforum.org

MEF is a think tank that works to define and promote American interests in the Middle East. MEF publishes the policy-oriented journal *Middle East Quarterly* and promotes numerous activities, including its director's Web site, DanielPipes.org, with many pages of writings, television transcripts, and testimony. The MEF Web site provides links to *Middle East Quarterly* and MEF articles, audio recordings, summary accounts of addresses by top experts, and more.

U.S. Department of State Bureau of Near Eastern Affairs
2201 C St. NW, Washington, DC   20520
(202) 647-4000
Web site: www.state.gov/p/nea/

The bureau deals with U.S. foreign policy and U.S. relations with the countries in the Middle East and North Africa, including Israel. Its Web site offers country information, as well as news briefings and press statements on U.S. foreign policy.

World Jewish Congress (WJC)
501 Madison Ave., New York, NY   10022
(212) 755-5770
e-mail: info@worldjewishcongress.org
Web site: www.worldjewishcongress.org

The World Jewish Congress is an international organization that addresses the interests and needs of Jews and Jewish communities worldwide. Its publications include an official newsletter, the "World Jewish Congress Report," and the quarterly *Israel Journal of Foreign Affairs* as well as monthly dispatches, Policy Forum reports, and Policy Studies. The WJC Web site features online community forums, opinion polls, and articles and videos on topics of concern to the Jewish community.

Zionist Organization of America (ZOA)
4 E. Thirty-fourth St., New York, NY   10016
(212) 481-1500 • fax: (212) 481-1515
e-mail: info@zoa.org
Web site: www.zoa.org

ZOA is the oldest, and one of the largest, pro-Israel organizations in the United States. It works to strengthen U.S.-Israeli relations through educational activities, public affairs programs, and by combating anti-Israel bias in the media, textbooks, and on campuses. ZOA publications include the twice yearly *ZOA Report*, which can be downloaded from the ZOA Web site. The Web site also provides news and updates, action alerts, op-eds and special reports, and links to articles in the *Jerusalem Post*.

Bibliography of Books

Bernard Avishai   *The Hebrew Republic: How Secular
                   Democracy and Global Enterprise Will
                   Bring Israel Peace at Last.* Orlando,
                   FL: Houghton Mifflin Harcourt,
                   2008.

Shlomo Ben-Ami   *Scars of War, Wounds of Peace: The
                  Israeli-Arab Tragedy.* New York:
                  Oxford University Press, 2006.

Jimmy Carter   *Palestine: Peace Not Apartheid.* New
                  York: Simon & Schuster, 2006.

Jimmy Carter   *We Can Have Peace in the Holy Land:
                  A Plan That Will Work.* New York:
                  Simon & Schuster, 2009.

Rich Cohen   *Israel Is Real: An Obsessive Quest to
                  Understand the Jewish Nation and Its
                  History.* New York: Farrar, Straus &
                  Giroux, 2009.

Alan Dershowitz   *The Case Against Israel's Enemies.*
                  Hoboken, NJ: Wiley, 2008.

Alan Dershowitz   *What Israel Means to Me: By 80
                  Prominent Writers, Performers,
                  Scholars, Politicians, and Journalists.*
                  Hoboken, NJ: Wiley, 2006.

Abraham H.   *The Deadliest Lies: The Israel Lobby
Foxman   and the Myth of Jewish Control.* New
                  York: Palgrave Macmillan, 2007.

Caroline B. Glick *Shackled Warrior: Israel and the
                   Global Jihad.* New York: Gefen, 2008.

| Galia Golan | *Israel and Palestine: Peace Plans and Proposals from Oslo to Disengagement.* Princeton, NJ: Markus Wiener, 2007. |

Dore Gold — *The Fight for Jerusalem: Radical Islam, the West, and the Future of the Holy City.* Washington, DC: Regnery, 2007.

Jeffrey Goldberg — *Prisoners: A Muslim and a Jew Across the Middle East Divide.* New York: Knopf, 2006.

Constance Hilliard — *Does Israel Have a Future? The Case for a Post-Zionist State.* Dulles, VA: Potomac Books, 2009.

Martin Indyk — *Innocent Abroad: An Intimate Account of American Peace Diplomacy in the Middle East.* New York: Simon & Schuster, 2009.

Efraim Karsh and Rory Miller, eds. — *Israel at Sixty: Rethinking the Birth of the Jewish State.* London: Routledge, 2008.

Daniel C. Kurtzer and Scott B. Lasensky — *Negotiating Arab-Israeli Peace: American Leadership in the Middle East.* Washington, DC: United Institute of Peace Press, 2008.

Saree Makdisi — *Palestine Inside Out: An Everyday Occupation.* New York: Norton, 2008.

Aaron David Miller — *The Much Too Promised Land: America's Elusive Search for Arab-Israeli Peace.* New York: Bantam Dell, 2008.

Benny Morris   *One State, Two States: Resolving the*
                        Israel/Palestine Conflict. New Haven,
                        CT: Yale University Press, 2009.

Kenneth M.   *A Path Out of the Desert: A Grand*
Pollack   *Strategy for America in the Middle*
                        East. New York: Random House,
                        2008.

Jīhān Sādāt   *My Hope for Peace.* New York: Free
                        Press, 2009.

Shlomo Sand   *The Invention of the Jewish People.*
                        London: Verso, 2009.

Avi Shlaim   *Israel and Palestine: Reflections,*
                        Revisions, Refutations. London: Verso,
                        2009.

Sandy Tolan   *The Lemon Tree: an Arab, a Jew, and*
                        the Heart of the Middle East. New
                        York: Bloomsbury, 2006.

Bernard   *Divided Jerusalem: The Struggle for*
Wasserstein   *the Holy Land.* New Haven, CT: Yale
                        University Press, 2008.

Marcus   *Naïve & Abroad: Israel and Palestine,*
Henderson Wilder   *Obvious Questions No One Asks.*
                        Bloomington, IN: iUniverse, 2009.

Philip C. Winslow   *Victory for Us Is to See You Suffer: In*
                        the West Bank with the Palestinians
                        and the Israelis. Boston: Beacon,
                        2007.

| Alexander Yakobson and Amnon Rubinstein | *Israel and the Family of Nations: The Jewish Nation State and Human Rights*. London: Routledge, 2009. |

Index

ML   1/11